KHARKOV 1943

A lost victory for the Panzers?

Philippe NAUD

Layout by Antonin Collet
Maps by Philippe Naud and Antonin Collet
Color Plate by Jean Restayn
Translation from French by Lawrence Brown
Collection Editor Nicolas Stratigos

Histoire & Collections

KHARKOV 1943
A LOST VICTORY?

A battery of Katyusha rocket launchers opens fire on the "fascists". The rocket salvoes were the final phase of the Red Army's artillery preparation throughout the 1942-1943 offensives. (DR).

By 1943, things were looking decidedly better for the USSR. Indeed, the Red Army had regained the initiative against a weakened Ostheer, the German Army in the east that had begun to accumulate a series of reversals. Admittedly, on the Leningrad sector, Operation "Iskra" (spark), had, only by mid-January, opened a narrow corridor to the city without lifting the siege. Also, the November offensive launched to reduce the Rzhev salient (Operation March) ended in a bloodbath. However, things were much different in the area of the Don. Firstly, Operation Uranus, also launched in November, was much more successful than had been hoped for and had trapped the German 6.Armee in Stalingrad. Then, in December, Operation Maly Saturn (small Saturn) led to the destruction of the Italian 8a Armata on the Don and forced the Nazi high command to definitively abandon any hope of holding Stalingrad. Maly Saturn ruined the German relief operation for the 6.Armee, "Wintergewitter" (winter storm).

Also ruined were any hopes for air supplies as, on 24 December, the T-34 tanks of the 24th Corps broke through from the Don and overran the Tatsinskaya airfield, forcing the German planes to take off and escape. At the end of December, Manstein's Panzers, sent to help the 6.Armee, also had to escape with the Red Army hot on their heels. The Ju-52 transport planes had to take off from airfields that were even farther away from the Stalingrad Kessel, and the already overstretched air bridge collapsed. Another consequence was that of the withdrawal, starting on the 28th, of Heeresgruppe A (Army group), – HG A –, in the Caucasus, towards the Rostov bottleneck. Despite refusing to give up any ground, Hitler was forced to admit the seriousness of the situation. He promised reinforcements to the HG Don of Feldmarschall Manstein and to HG "B" of Feldmarschall Weichs, but by mid-January 1943, the entire Axis front south of Kursk was in pieces.

Indeed, the Soviet successes of the end of 1942 led to a new series of crushing victories following "Maly Saturn". On 13 January, the preliminary reconnaissance in force against the Hungarian 2nd Army of HG "B" on the Don obtained such a success that the Voronej

This Ju52/3m from KGzbV172 probably took part in the supplying of the Stalingrad pocket. This unsuccessful airlift cost almost 500 planes, of which 266 were Ju 52 transport aircraft. *(BA).*

This Kharkov boulevard seen here at the beginning of 1943 is used by horse-drawn and motorised elements. The esplanade visible in the background is in Constitution Square. *(BA).*

1 - *These were the two towns that formed the main objective of the offensive.*
2 - *These figures include the German 6.Armee that capitulated on 2 February.*

Front brought forward the "Ostrogozhsk-Rossosh"[1] offensive. As planned, the 2.Armee, the right flank of HG Mitte (centre), threatened by the Hungarian collapse, covered itself in the south before starting to withdraw towards Kursk on 27 January under pressure from the Briansk Front. Two 2.Armee Army Corps, encircled to the west of Voronej, only managed to escape because the deep snow was as much of a handicap to the Soviets as it was to the Germans! The retreat continued and the Stavka the Red Army high command, and above all Stalin, thought that total victory was within their grasp. Since November, the Axis in the southern sector had suffered losses of 600,000 men killed or taken prisoner, and six armies, two of which were German, had been decimated leaving the Dnieper as apparent the only line on which to make a stand[2]. Thus, on 23 January, the Vojd (guide) decided to launch a series of vast operations to transform this retreat from Russia into a rout. Not all Generals shared Stalin's enthusiasm, especially given the fact that the mechanised forces were worn down and that the resistance of the German 6.Armee in Stalingrad immobilised several infantry armies. Stalin would not listen to these warnings, and with accompanying attacks

on the flanks, the Stavka ordered two new offensives in the southern sector of the USSR. Operation Skachok (gallop), led by Vatutin's south west front, was to retake Dobas, operating alongside "mobile group Popov", an improvised tank Army, and push the Germans back to the Dnieper, or even farther... Nobody thought that Berlin could be reached by the end of the year. The second offensive, Zvezda (star), was to liberate Kharkov, the second largest city in the Ukraine, contributing to the success of "Skachok" of which it was an offshoot. For the third time since 1941, the Ukrainian city would find itself at the heart of military operations of the Great Patriotic War.

In 1941, with a population of 850,000, Kharkov was the fourth largest city in the Soviet Union. The capital of the Ukraine until 1934, as its population was more "Russian" than Kiev, the city had only been founded in the 17th century. It was rapidly industrialised in the 1930s under the impulse of Stalinist policies. Armaments were an important part of its industrial output, and its factories were the first to produce, starting in June 1940, the famous T-34 tank. The catastrophic defeat of the Red Army around Kiev in September 1941

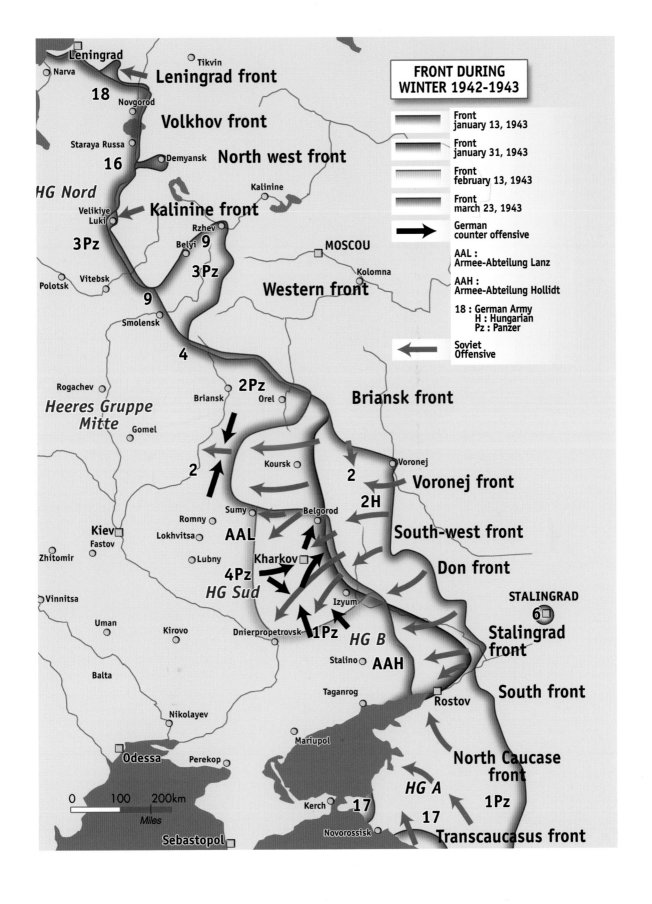

FRONT DURING
WINTER 1942-1943

Front
january 13, 1943

Front
january 31, 1943

Front
february 13, 1943

Front
march 23, 1943

German
counter offensive

AAL :
Armee-Abteilung Lanz

AAH :
Armee-Abteilung Hollidt

18 : German Army
H : Hungarian
Pz : Panzer

Soviet
Offensive

Leningrad
Narva
Tikvin
Leningrad front
18
Novgorod
Volkhov front
Staraya Russa
Demyansk
North west front
16
HG Nord
Kalinine
Velikiye Luki
Kalinine front
3Pz
Rzhev
Belyi
9
3Pz
MOSCOU
Kolomna
9
Polotsk
Vitebsk
Western front
Smolensk
4
Rogachev
Heeres Gruppe Mitte
2Pz
Gomel
Briansk
Orel
Brisank front
Koursk
Voronej
2
2
Voronej front
Sumy
Belgorod
2H
Romny
AAL
South-west front
Kiev
Lokhvitsa
Fastov
Lubny
Kharkov
Don front
Zhitomir
4Pz
HG Sud
STALINGRAD
Vinnitsa
Izyum
6
Uman
Kirovo
1Pz
HG B
Stalingrad front
Dnierpropetrovsk
Stalino
AAH
Balta
South front
Taganrog
Rostov
Nikolayev
Odessa
Perekop
Mariupol
North Caucase front
0   100   200km
HG A
1Pz
Miles
Kerch
17
17
Sebastopol
Novorossisk
Transcaucasus front

General Golikov was commander of the Voronezh Front tasked with taking Kharkov, known as Operation "Zveszda". He was aware of the scale of the task, but his superior officers were still caught up in the euphoria of the victories achieved at the end of 1942 and beginning of 1943. (DR).

allowed the Germans to reach Kharkov in October. However, the autumn raspoutitsa – the "season without roads" – slowed down the German advance and allowed most of the factories to be evacuated or destroyed[3]. Kharkov fell to the 6.Armee on 25 October. The city was subjected to the horrors of Nazi occupation, and, despite the difficulties of the winter campaign, the military helped Einsatzgruppe C to shoot or gas 20,000 Jews between December and January[4].

Although non-Jewish Ukrainians and Russians escaped systematic extermination, many were murdered in reprisal against the first partisan operations, deported to Germany for labour, or fell victim to famine as most of the harvests were sent to the Reich. A Soviet eye-witness stated that during the winter, there were "no food stocks, no markets, no shops".

By January 1942, the population of Kharkov had fallen to 300,000. Having become an important logistical centre for the Ostheer, the town was later relatively spared. In May, an offensive by the southwest front to retake the city was a disaster and did not even reach the suburbs. Columns of Soviet prisoners were loaded onto trains at the station and left for German camps. However, at the beginning of 1943, events were very different, the Red Army had gone from victory to victory since November the previous year.

3 - *The Kharkov military district also formed 28 Rifle divisions.*

4 - *Gassing was undertaken with modified trucks. 14,000 people were murdered in January alone.*

5 - *A "Front" designates here a group of armies, smaller in size than their German counterparts. There were thirteen fronts in February 1943.*

6 - *60% of the 211,000 soldiers of the 2nd Hungarian Army were killed, wounded, taken prisoner or posted as missing between 12 January and the end of February.*

THE OPPONENTS
THE RED ARMY AT THE BATTLE OF KHARKOV

The main thrust fell to the Voronezh Front commanded by General Golikov, at that time more than 100 km from Kharkov[5].

Formed in July 1942, the Voronezh Front undertook attacks around the city that were as vain as they were murderous, before proving themselves during Operation Ostrogozhsk-Rossosh that eliminated the Hungarian 2nd Army and decimated the Italian Alpine Corps and the few German divisions present in the sector[6]. As a reward, some units received the title of "Guards", such as the 7th Cavalry Corps which became the 6th Guards Corps. Losses were sustainable, with those

End of January 1943, the Italian Alpine Corps retreating with assault guns probably belonging to Sturmgeschütze-Abteilung.190. (BA).

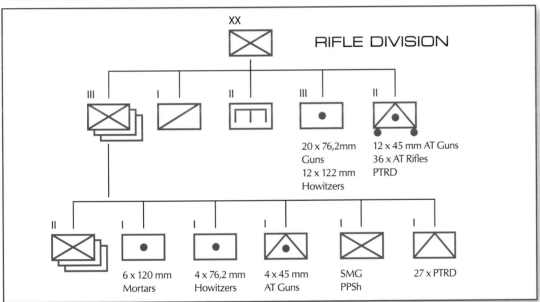

XX

RIFLE DIVISION

III — I — II — III — II

20 x 76,2mm Guns
12 x 122 mm Howitzers

12 x 45 mm AT Guns
36 x AT Rifles PTRD

II — I — I — I — I — I

6 x 120 mm Mortars

4 x 76,2 mm Howitzers

4 x 45 mm AT Guns

SMG PPSh

27 x PTRD

Notes : 1. This is a theoretical organisation chart : 9,435 men, 204 guns and mortars.

2. Guards divisions were issued with more equipment and men – 10,670 in theory. A standard division, for example, had 434 light machine-guns, whereas a guards division had 490, but these differences did not appear during the offensive towards Kharkov.

for the Rifle Divisions reaching 65% or more of their theoretical strength. However, Golikov, also involved in the offensive against the 2.Armee of HG Mitte, could only use the 40th and 69th armies, the latter only just having been created from the 18th Rifle Corps, and the 3rd Guards tank Army for Operation Zvezda[7]. Indeed, on 26 Janaury, the success of the Briansk Front led the Stavska to include Kursk in the Golikov objectives. Deprived of its 38th and 60th armies, it was also lacking most of its heavy artillery, stationed at the east of the Don, but this did not matter as the Germans were withdrawing. Luckily, reinforcements, including two Tank Corps, were due to arrive. "Zvezda", planned to start on 1 February, was delayed by 24 hours in order

to allow the Voronezh Front to concentrate its forces. The latter was comprised of nearly 200,000 men and 300 tanks. Opposing them, the Soviets correctly estimated that there were only decimated units and that they largely outnumbered them in men and especially in tanks. However, they were convinced that the mechanised columns around Kharkov were in retreat despite the fact that most were heading towards the city or the east. To sum up, the forces comprising the Voronezh Front appeared to be adequate, despite attrition, particularly in the mechanised units, after three weeks of winter fighting and movement. The title of "Guards" had not immediately led to any extra weapons or personnel. Also, the 40th Army commanded

7 - An order of battle for the Soviets at the beginning of "Zvezda" is found on page 81.

This knocked out Valentine is a reminder that the western allies supplied a large number of the tanks used by the Red Army during this period of the war. Well-liked by the men who used them, unlike the American tanks, more than 3,800 of these tanks, nick-named the "Pyps" (puppy) were delivered between 1941 and 1944. (BA).

8 - *General Kravchenko's 4th Corps became the "5th guards Corps" on 7 February 1943 due to its success of "Uranus" and against the 2nd Hungarian Army.*

9 - *It should be remembered that although the Allied aid in the form of "Lend-Lease" was primarily American, the British and Canadians also made a great contribution. The Valentine tank, made in both of the latter countries, was very well-liked by its Soviet crews.*

by General Moskalenko planned to use 40% of its infantry to reduce pockets of resistance along with the 5th Guards Tank Corps limited to 30% of its theoretical tank strength![8] As for the 3rd Tank Army led by General Rybalko, it was also suffering from the wear and tear of operations with two-thirds of its tanks unserviceable, mostly due to break downs. The only unit that was almost complete was the 6th Guards Cavalry Corps, the "mobile" infantry of Rybalko's two Tank Corps, but which lacked any "punch" and limited to two divisions rather than the three that was usually the case.

Finally, some independent Tank Regiments and Brigades were reduced to ten Tanks.

What about the Red Army at the beginning of 1943? It was no longer the powerful, resilient, but clumsy mass that had been hit by "Barbarossa" in the summer of 1941. Despite the loss of industrial cities such as Kharkov, it now received large deliveries of armaments, with the latter theoretically being more widely distributed, such as 12 light-machine guns per infantry company compared to 9 at the end of 1941. Thus, the Rifle Divisions underwent a new table of organisation and equipment starting in December 1942 and which hardly varied until the end of the war. Industry was now up to full speed; the USSR produced more than 2,000 45 mm anti-tank guns in 1941 and by 1942 this figure had been multiplied by ten and with a more powerful gun. As for the tanks, the "Tankograd" complex at Chelyabinsk in the Urals was in full production. From January to March 1942, more than 1,600 T-34 tanks rolled off the production lines. This number was almost tripled during the first half or third of the year. Over the year, the USSR made 12,500 T-34 tanks alone, whereas the Reich produced only 6,000 Panzers, Sturmgeschütze and Panzerjäger. For the Russians, we also have to add 10,600 light tanks and more than 2,400 heavy KV tanks. One must not forget the important contribution of the Allies in supplying transport vehicles. Motorised infantry units used Jeeps, Ford and Studebaker vehicles[9].

Army structure also evolved. Small armies comprising of Infantry Divisions and Tank Brigades, relatively flexible but ill-suited to large mobile operations, gave way to more complex formations. The tank Corps that appeared at the beginning of 1942, sometimes ended up as armies such as that of Rybalko. There were three others, each with at least two armoured

Corps and other support units. As for the Rifle Divisions, they were sometimes regrouped into Corps that had disappeared during 1941. They allowed for a better coordination of support troops, tanks, engineers, artillery, etc. that were themselves becoming more numerous. At a higher echelon, Army Artillery Regiments had grown more than two-fold between the start and end of 1942, and 18 Artillery Divisions appeared to coordinate this enormous mass of artillery pieces. Two of these served on the Voronezh Front. Air forces saw an improvement in tactics, such as fighters operating in pairs, as well as better planes, of either Soviet or Allied manufacture. They were at last able to challenge the Luftwaffe for air superiority, especially as the latter had been ground down by the Stalingrad campaign. The Cavalry, the only mobile component of the Red Army as 1941 led into 1942, and in theory obsolete, saw its less numerous Corps become more powerful with the addition of tanks and artillery.

However, like the Cavalry, which was still very vulnerable to Panzers and the Luftwaffe, the Red Army went through a transitional period. The Tank Armies, like that of Rybalko, were not comparable to the German Panzerkorps as they were handicapped by the presence of slow and vulnerable infantry and Cavalry.

The latter made up for the weakness of motorised riflemen. The creation of mechanised Corps with more infantry still came up against the lack of trucks, despite the deliveries of Allied trucks. The same applied to the artillery of the mobile Corps, limited to a few mortars and 76.2 mm guns, despite the famous Katyushas or "Guards mortars" that were as powerful as they were inaccurate. Finally, the Red Army did not yet sufficiently master large mobile operations; its winter successes had been achieved against the allies of the Reich that were lacking in motivation, poorly equipped and/or commanded, and rendered punch-drunk by the massed artillery that was unable to follow a mobile offensive. Command and control, more competent and subjected less to NKVD control, retained its old habits of frontal attack rather than manoeuvre, something that was more difficult due to a deficiency in transmissions, notably in tanks. Faced with better trained German tank crews, fighting often turned to the advantage of the Panzers. Finally, logistics suffered from too distant base depots and lines of communication that were already mediocre and partially destroyed. In January, many of

The T-34 remained, and quite rightly so, the favourite tank used by Soviet crews. The tank seen here belonged to the 96th Brigade, one of the independent armoured units placed at the disposal of the Voronezh Front, most of which were a long way off having the regulation number of 53 tanks! (DR).

Notes : *1. This is a theoretical organisation chart : 1,038 men, 32 T-34, 21 T-70 and 126 other vehicles (trucks, cars, tractors etc.).*

2. There were many variations in tank equipment.

3. As with other organisation charts, non-combatant units and staff units are not shown in order to simplify.

Notes : *1. This is a theoretical organisation chart : 7,853 men, 170 tanks (including eight in reserve), 78 mortars and light artillery pieces, eight multiple rocket-launchers, 24 anti-aircraft guns, etc.*

2. Corps support units such as anti-aircraft battalions or motorised Rifle Brigades are not always present. In theory, the latter also had three support companies-anti-tank, Ppsh SMG and reconnaissance.

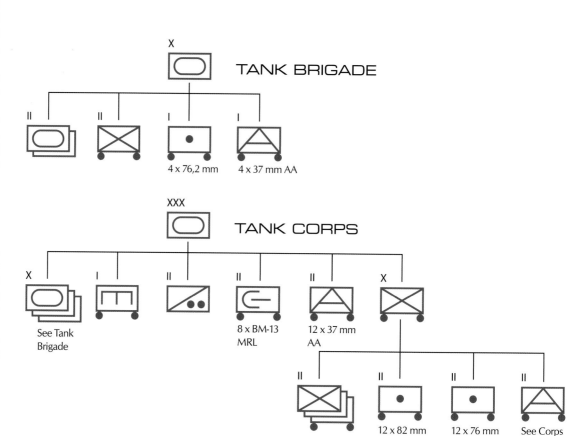

TANK BRIGADE

4 x 76,2 mm   4 x 37 mm AA

TANK CORPS

See Tank Brigade

8 x BM-13 MRL   12 x 37 mm AA

12 x 82 mm 6 x 120 mm Mortars   12 x 76 mm Guns   See Corps

T34 1943 Model unknown unit, Voronej Front, Kharkov, February 1943.

these depots were still east of the Don. However, these weaknesses appeared secondary within the victorious context. The Frontoviki saw the long lines of prisoners, the wrecks and slaughterhouses that bore witness to the defeat of the Axis forces, and finally, the joy of the populations that, even if they had not enjoyed life under Stalin, were happy to see the end of the "new order", albeit short-lived in eastern Ukraine.

So, in front of Kharkov, what could the Ostheer do faced with the armies of Golikov?

ARMEEABTEILUNG LANZ AND THE SS-PANZERKORPS

Indeed, only one "Army detachment" (Armeeabteilung) faced the Voronezh Front.

Created on 1 February 1943 from the German General staff attached to the Italian 8a Armata, the group commanded by General der Gebirgstruppe Lanz was tasked within HG "B", with protecting Kharkov and the northern flank of HG Don. Upon Hitler's orders, the city became a fortress and therefore something that would not be abandoned. Firstly, Lanz had to hold the Oskol River line that was already often crossed by elements of the Voronezh Front. However, as its name suggests, this "Armeeabteilung" was no more than an improvised force stripped of most of the means allocated to a real Army, such as services and organic units like artillery, engineers, flak and so on[10]. Its two Sturmgeschütze groups were mere shadows of their former selves and soon left the front due to a lack of materiel! In order to carry out his impossible missions, Lanz had at his disposal all or part of seven German Infantry Divisions, most of which had been decimated during the January battles, as well as the remains of a few Hungarian units of dubious military value, including one armoured division with ten tanks...

In any case, the remains of the 2nd Army withdrew to Hungary in the days that followed. The movement of the Golikov Front did not escape the attention of the Germans as, contrary to the offensives undertaken up to that point in time, the confident Russians did not use the Maskirovka technique of camouflage and concealment in order to hide their preparations. Faced with the

10 - *The composition of Armeeabteilung Lanz is shown on page 81.*

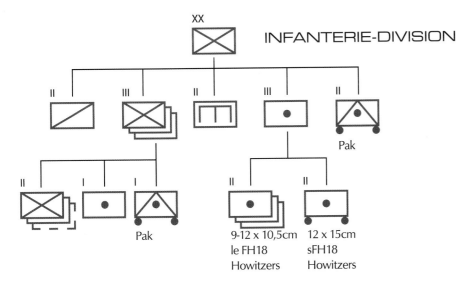

INFANTERIE-DIVISION

Pak

Pak

9-12 x 10,5cm le FH18 Howitzers

12 x 15cm sFH18 Howitzers

Infanterie-Sturmabzeichen
(German insignia of Infantry combat).
(DR).

Notes : This is a theoretical organisation chart.

1. Few divisions had three infantry battalions per regiment.

2. The PaK were often PaK 38, the 7,5 cm PaK 40 were rare and the old PaK 35/36 were still used. Many units used captured guns, such as the well-liked Russian 76.2 mm gun. Self-propelled anti-tank guns were very rare.

3. Regimental artillery companies mostly used 7,5 cm and 15 cm howitzers, but it was not uncommon for them to use captured Russian guns.

4. Some divisions combined their reconnaissance group, in general cyclists, and their anti-tank group into a partially motorised "Schnelle Abteilung" (rapid group).

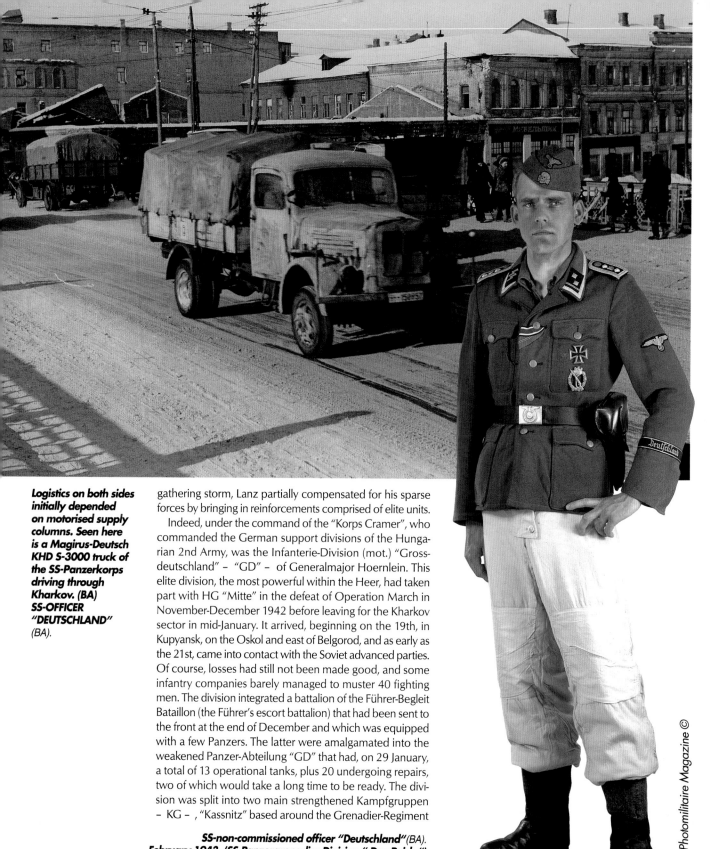

Logistics on both sides initially depended on motorised supply columns. Seen here is a Magirus-Deutsch KHD S-3000 truck of the SS-Panzerkorps driving through Kharkov. (BA)
SS-OFFICER "DEUTSCHLAND" (BA).

gathering storm, Lanz partially compensated for his sparse forces by bringing in reinforcements comprised of elite units.

Indeed, under the command of the "Korps Cramer", who commanded the German support divisions of the Hungarian 2nd Army, was the Infanterie-Division (mot.) "Grossdeutschland" – "GD" – of Generalmajor Hoernlein. This elite division, the most powerful within the Heer, had taken part with HG "Mitte" in the defeat of Operation March in November-December 1942 before leaving for the Kharkov sector in mid-January. It arrived, beginning on the 19th, in Kupyansk, on the Oskol and east of Belgorod, and as early as the 21st, came into contact with the Soviet advanced parties. Of course, losses had still not been made good, and some infantry companies barely managed to muster 40 fighting men. The division integrated a battalion of the Führer-Begleit Bataillon (the Führer's escort battalion) that had been sent to the front at the end of December and which was equipped with a few Panzers. The latter were amalgamated into the weakened Panzer-Abteilung "GD" that had, on 29 January, a total of 13 operational tanks, plus 20 undergoing repairs, two of which would take a long time to be ready. The division was split into two main strengthened Kampfgruppen – KG – , "Kassnitz" based around the Grenadier-Regiment

***SS-non-commissioned officer "Deutschland"**(BA).*
February 1943. (SS-Panzergrenadier-Division " Das Reich ")

As was often the case, the Luftwaffe, Wehrmacht or SS flak units played an important role in ground fighting. Despite their vulnerability, the 88, such as the one seen here, was very successful in an anti-tank role. (BA).

and "Lorenz" built around the "Fusilier-Regiment"[11]. This tired but formidable "GD" reinforcement included a StuG-Abteilung – which meant that Lanz had at his disposal, between Kupyansk and Novy Oskol, a line some 150 km in length, only 50,000 German soldiers and fifty Panzers. Opposing them were nearly 200,000 men and 300 tanks, but Lanz would be able to count on another powerful reinforcement.

On 31 December 1942, Hitler promised Manstein the new SS-Panzerkorps in order to help the 6.Armee to break out of Stalingrad[12]. The situation, deemed "serious" in November then became catastrophic. However, the transfer of this strong mechanised force from western Europe was delayed[13]. Also, as it was newly formed, it did not yet have all of its units, especially that of the SS-PanzerGrenadier-Division "Totenkopf", based in the Angoulême region to France and which was still undergoing training. However, the terminology should not mislead us. The only Nazi divisions to then have the title of "Panzer-Grenadier", they were not motorised units with a few tanks, such as the Heer motorised divisions, but were reinforced Panzer-Divisionen, -each one having an extra 50% of infantry plus a Sturmgeschütze-Abteilung and one company of ten of the new heavy Tiger tanks.

The "GD" did not receive its Tigers until March![14] Reichsführer Himmler had personally ensured that his political soldiers received the best equipment, such as numerous 7.5 cm PaK 40 guns and a flak group armed with 88 mm guns that also excelled in an anti-tank role. The three divisions of SS-Obergruppenführer Hausser also arrived rested and fresh, something that could not be said for the Ostheer formations such as the "GD".

Wiped out during "Barbarossa", they came back at the beginning of 1943, fully manned, well led, experienced and well trained, apart from the "Totenkopf" which left the USSR in autumn 1942, hastily finishing its over-haul. Only the "LAH" and "Das Reich", comprisd of 38,000 men and nearly 250 tanks and assault guns, began reach to Kharkov at the end of January, followed by the "Totenkopf"[15]. Not having managed to save Stalingrad, Hitler hoped that his praetorian guard would be able to hold on to Kharkov.

Although they had been suffering from the blows of the Red Army since mid-November, the Germans kept a cool head and had no intention of retreating to the Dnieper. Despite the worrying situation of his HG "Don", Manstein was already contemplating a major counter-offensive with the arrival of the first reinforcements. The most important requirement remained that of re-establishing the front and

11 - "KG" signifies "tactical grouping" first of all, but it is also used for a decimated division, reduced to an inter-arm grouping. A KG Generally bears the name of its commander
12 - Hitler refused to abandon Stalingrad and wanted the 6.Armee to hold out until the spring.
13 - The "LAH" took part in the invasion of the non-occupied region of France.
14 - The composition of the SS divisions is on page 20.
15 - Some units arrived at a fairly late stage, such as Das Reich StuG-Abt, at the end of February.

making sure that the HG A could escape the Caucasus via Rostov. Hitler, despite his hostility towards ceding terrain, accepted on 27 January to withdraw the 1.Pz. Armee from the Caucasus in order to support HG "Don". However, once more, these were weakened formations and at the same time, he ordered preparations for a limited counter-offensive in the Kharkov region with the SS-Panzerkorps. When "Skachok" began on the 29th, with the obvious objective of retaking Donbas, he did not cancel this project whilst a large part of Hausser's men were still en route, and with the "Totenkopf" not due to arrive before 31 January! Hitler was also stubborn concerning one point; Kharkov would not be another Stalingrad and must be held at all costs.

Here again, the Red Army was faster than the Nazis.

BATTLES TO THE EAST OF KHARKOV
A "STAR" IS BORN....

With Hausser's Corps arriving little by little, Golikov was already driving towards Kharkov.

His orders were to destroy enemy forces to the west before taking the city, opening a gap in the "fascist" lines[16]. His 38th and 60th armies headed towards Kursk whilst also protecting his right flank. The 40th Army pushed towards Belgorod which it passed by on

7 February by turning towards the south in order to encircle Kharkov by the west and north-west. Moskalenko hoped to quickly retrieve his units busy clearing pockets of resistance to his rear, which included his Tank Corps, in order to send them forward. The 69th Army, commanded by General Kasakov, Golikov's Chief-of-Staff, had a fairly straightforward mission that consisted of coming from the north-east and capturing crossing points over the Donets, then carrying on towards Kharkov.

As for Rybalko, flanked to the south by Vatutin's 6th Army, he attacked towards the west and through the Donets reaching Moskalenko on the 7th in order to encircle the last enemy forces before reaching Kharkov. The Oskol, already crossed in several sectors, was a less tricky obstacle than the Donets, especially as the west bank was higher. The fairly flat terrain was not very wooded and comprised of several small rivers and towns, some of which were fairly large, such as Belgorod, that were important to lines of communication as they were important road junctions within what was a poor road network. Golikov and his subordinates worried about the state of their forces and initially engaged most of their forces in order to gain a rapid victory. However, Rybalko, wishing to spare his weak armoured Corps, sent in ahead his riflemen and Cavalry (only 165 of his 300 tanks were operational on 29 January). "Zvezda" began on 2 February without any preliminary artillery

16 - The Soviets preferred to talk of "Fascists" or "Hitlerite-Fascists" rather than Nazis.

17 - It should be remembered that the last units of the 6.Armee capitulated the same day at Stalingrad.

preparation due to a lack of guns and shells[17]. In fact, reconnaissance in strength had begun the day before. The Germans, alerted by the start of "Skachok" on 29 January, saw near Izium in the south the 320th Infantry Division collapse against the 6th Army. They awaited the 3rd Tank Army that had achieved minor successes. North of Kupyansk, two battalions of the "Deutschland" regiment (Das Reich) blocked the riflemen. The following day, a little farther north, the 201st Tank Brigade broke through against a police regiment and opened the way for the 6th Guards Cavalry Corps. The same applied to Rybalko's left flank, where his riflemen took on other elements of the 213.Sicherungs-Division. The size of the area to defend and its wide open spaces prevented the SS from offering an effective defence everywhere.

The "Deutschland" motorcyclist 15.Kompanie came to the assistance of the police but was unable to plug the gap, despite the help of part of the "LAH" SS-Pz. Gre.Rgt.1. Also, around Kupyansk, the 111th Division was giving the German 298th Infantry Division a hard time, despite here too the support of SS detachments. The presence of the latter bothered Rybalko who, in order to catch them off-guard, decided to send in his two tank Corps the next day behind his Cavalry. Advancing in two echelons, they were to take

crossing points on the Donets by advancing at least twenty kilometres per day. However, on the same 3 February, "LAH" reinforcements began entering into the fighting, and although Rybalko's four units skirted the frozen Donets near Petchenegi, less than 30 km from Kharkov, they came up against the SS everywhere.

An officer serving with the "LAH" described their success : "*Firstly, we had a counter-attack force sufficiently strong behind our positions that were very*

Stalingrad, 2 February 1943, Feldmarschall Paulus is about to sign his Army's capitulation, a major turning point of the war. However, the fierce German resistance in this "Kessel" helped the defenders of Kharkov by pinning down large Soviet forces. (DR).

The T-70 was the standard light tank of the Red Army. Outclassed by virtually all of the Panzers, they made up more than a third of the tank Corps' armoured vehicles. (DR).

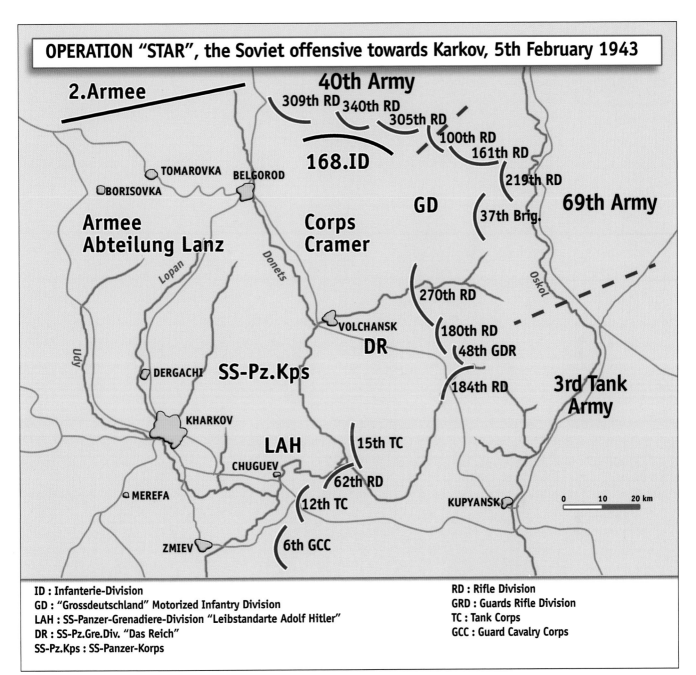

OPERATION "STAR", the Soviet offensive towards Karkov, 5th February 1943

2.Armee

40th Army

309th RD   340th RD

305th RD

100th RD

161th RD

219th RD

168.ID

GD

69th Army

37th Brig.

TOMAROVKA   BELGOROD

BORISOVKA

Armee
Abteilung Lanz

Corps
Cramer

Lopan

Donets

Oskol

270th RD

VOLCHANSK

DR

180th RD

48th GDR

Udy

DERGACHI

SS-Pz.Kps

184th RD

3rd Tank
Army

KHARKOV

LAH

15th TC

CHUGUEV

62th RD

MEREFA

12th TC

KUPYANSK

0   10   20 km

ZMIEV

6th GCC

ID : Infanterie-Division
GD : "Grossdeutschland" Motorized Infantry Division
LAH : SS-Panzer-Grenadiere-Division "Leibstandarte Adolf Hitler"
DR : SS-Pz.Gre.Div. "Das Reich"
SS-Pz.Kps : SS-Panzer-Korps

RD : Rifle Division
GRD : Guards Rifle Division
TC : Tank Corps
GCC : Guard Cavalry Corps

much established in depth... Secondly, we had two MG 42 per combat group and which we used for the first time with devastating effect". Also, the SS sent in a few armoured units such as the 3.Kompanie of the "LAH" reconnaissance group, against the 6th Cavalry Corps. The small Sdkfz 250 vehicles had no trouble travelling along the snow covered roads and engaged in a veritable "ride of death", machine-gunning the surprised horse-drawn columns. In the village of Korobotcheno, the Guards awaited them with machine-guns and anti-tank guns. The two leading troops lost two thirds of their number before withdrawing! Lanz, like Manstein, was against the more ambitious plans of attack proposed by Hausser, and feared that his Corps would be worn down too soon and before being able to use its full force in a real counter-offensive. However, the Armeeabteilung received an order from Hitler himself for a massive action with the SS-Panzerkorps towards the south in order to link up with the rest of the Manstein Army group. The start of "Zvezda" was more promising elsewhere. Indeed, Moskalenko and, in a lesser way,

Unlike the light tanks, the heavy KV tanks became rare and were no longer used in mobile Corps but in independent regiments allocated to a troop support role. (DR).

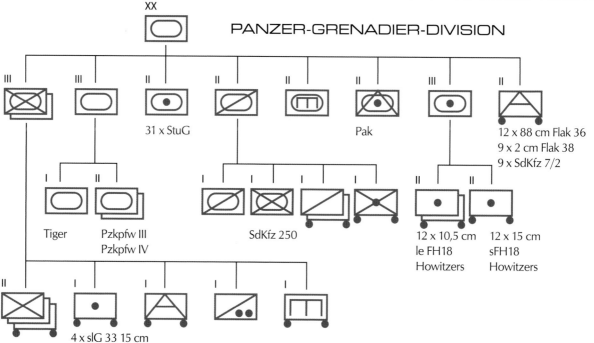

PANZER-GRENADIER-DIVISION

31 x StuG

Pak

12 x 88 cm Flak 36
9 x 2 cm Flak 38
9 x SdKfz 7/2

Tiger

Pzkpfw III
Pzkpfw IV

SdKfz 250

12 x 10,5 cm
le FH18
Howitzers

12 x 15 cm
sFH18
Howitzers

4 x sIG 33 15 cm

Notes : 1. This is a theoretical organisation chart but which applies, with some variations, to the SS-Panzerkorps units as well as the "GD" that was still known as an "Infanterie-Division (motorisiert)".

2. SS divisions had a strength of between 17,000 and 21,000 men, due to the presence, or not, of certain components. The "Totenkopf" thus had an extra two- battalion "rapid" regiment.

3. Initially, the "GD" only had one Panzer-Abteilung and no Panzer-Regiment, nor did it even have Tiger tanks.

4. One of the six Panzergrenadiere battalions was mechanised – "gepanzert"-, using Sdkfz 251, but not within the "GD".

5. The composition of the Flak-Abteilung is just to give an idea and corresponds to that of the "Totenkopf". Anti-tank or reconnaissance groups also differed greatly depending on divisions. Each division had at least one mechanised reconnaissance company equipped with Sdkfz 250.

The arrival of SS units around Kharkov meant that fresh combat units could be rapidly sent to the Voronezh Front. This radio Sdkfz 250/3 belonged to the "Das Reich" division. (BA).

Kazakov took on the z.b.V. Cramer Corps, both very spread out and weakened, with the "GD" not covering all of the "hot spots".

At dawn on 2 February and in polar conditions, the Frontoviki of the 69th Army attacked to the west of Oskol and pushed on towards Voltchansk[18]. In the north, a foray by the KG Kassnitz came up against the Russian assault that it held up at the cost of a few Panzers. The "GD" then blocked the 161st and 219th divisions around Veliko-Mikhailovka until 4 February. However, farther south, the 180th and 270th Divisions pushed on, even creating a gap with their neighbouring units which Kasakov hastily plugged with his 37th Brigade. The Soviets encircled here the various positions held by the "GD", with the latter having to withdraw in order to avoid being encircled. But, on 4 February, the 180th Division came up against the reconnaissance group of the "Das Reich". As with the "LAH", the mobility and firepower of the half-tracks and armoured cars had a devastating effect on riflemen without tank support. As for Rybalko,

the advance of Kasakov virtually ground to a halt. The 69th Army also came up against the powerful "Deutschland" regiment that was holding a forward position that could have been used as a jumping off point for a counter-attack against Rybalko. Paradoxically, it was Moskalenko, who attacked later with a weaker force and who had to cover 70 km in three days for a relatively secondary task, who had the most success. At 9 o'clock on 3 February, his four forward Rifle Divisions got the better of the German 168th Infantry Division, with the latter forced to make an orderly withdrawal. The 40th Army covered nearly 20 km by the evening, and on the 5th, its left flank linked up with the 69th Army. Faced with the scale of the situation, Lanz, who had realised the size of the Soviet offensive, ordered Hoernlein to send the A.A. "GD", with some back-up, including 88 mm guns and KG Pohlman, from the Führer-Begleit-Bataillon, to help the 168th Infantry Division[19]. KG Lorenz had to follow. The important Belgorod crossroads seemed to be within the grasp of the 40th Army and was

18 - The "GD" war history states, naturally, that the Hungarians "ran away".

19 - KG Pohlmann : two infantry companies, seven Panzers and two anti-tank PaK 40.

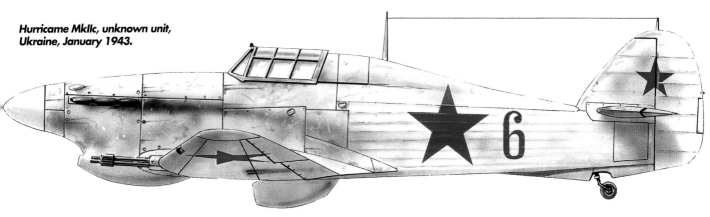

Hurricame MkIIc, unknown unit, Ukraine, January 1943.

The 10.5 cm FH 18 howitzer was the regulation artillery piece of the German divisional artillery. A heavy gun with a somewhat weak range, it nevertheless remained an accurate and formidable weapon. (BA).

This "88" is set-up in a typical ground fighting gun emplacement and appears to have an excellent field of fire. (BA).

clearly just a stage on the road to Kharkov. Despite the spectacular successes of Moskalenko, "Zvezda" was already behind schedule due to the unforeseen enemy resistance. It appeared that there would be difficult battles to come east of Kharkov and on the Donets.

Then, starting on 5 February, the German counter-attacks and Golikov's offensive bumped into each other.

ALL QUIET ON THE EASTERN FRONT?

Pushed on by his commander, Rybalko tried to efface the delays, whereas Hausser, also under pressure from his superiors, tried to regain the initiative.

However, the Germans were already in a delicate situation and saw their best units dispersed without being able to concentrate them. To his great despair, Lanz failed to make a decent reserve force due to the Russian offensive, even if Hausser's men carried out other "raids" to the east of Kupyansk against Rybalko's columns. The latter was furious at the problems encountered by his leading units. The previous day, the 195th Tank Brigade supported in vain an attempt by the riflemen of the 160th division faced with the Panzergrenadiere of the "LAH" to cross the Donets, when an SS "88" battery destroyed nine T-34 tanks, sometimes at a distance of more than 6 km (something which seems somewhat unbelievable). The commander of the 3rd tank Army was then forced to regroup its units on 5 February in order to try again the next day. The Russians

were happy to just probe the enemy lines, whereas the SS absorbed a group of the 298th I.D. that had managed to withdraw from the Kupyansk hornet's nest. Lanz and Hausser were particularly worried about the open right flank of the Armeeabteilung as "Skachok" was still in progress. The Russians were passing the Donets around Izioum and pushing back the 320th I.D., while the two tank Corps of the Popov group reached Slaviansk. Rybalko hoped to be able to exploit Lanz's left flank. With his superiors' agreement, he sent the 6th Cavalry Corps and his

Although this T-34 was not a victim of the previously seen gun, Soviet tank losses rose rapidly when "Zvezda" was launched, further weakening already under strength units. (BA).

Rarely used in such a role, turret-less T-60 light tanks are seen here towing 76.2 mm ZIS-3 guns, the excellent light artillery pieces used by the Red Army. Most Soviet units used trucks and horses to pull their artillery. (DR).

Unlike the ZIS-3, the German 7.5 cm leIG 18 was designed to be used in a direct infantry support role. The gun seen here with spoked wheels was therefore used by a regimental company. (BA).

Soviet citizens "offering" KV-1S tanks to Red Army soldiers. The fast "S" - Skorotsnoi KV was less armoured and partially equipped the 116th Brigade that liberated Belgorod. (DR).

20 - A "mobile group" was a mechanised formation that operated in front of a larger unit. Its job was to scout ahead, capture important road junctions and spread chaos and confusion. In theory, an Army was equipped with a tank Corps for this task.

broke through the lines held by the I./SS-Pz.Gre.Rgt.2. An immediate counter-attack, supported by StuG assault-guns and half-tracks armed with 2 cm anti-aircraft guns, hit the Russians before they had time to dig in and they were forced to withdraw with heavy losses. As for the 6th Cavalry Corps, they exploited the gaps created by the retreat of the 298th Infantry Division, and at nightfall, infiltrated behind the 201st Brigade. The success of Dietrich's men did not in any way erase the gravity of the situation for the Germans.

Whilst trying to save the survivors of the 298.ID and 320.ID, Lanz sped up preparations for the defence of Kharkov, with this role being devolved to the 213.Sich. Div. Heavy flak batteries were set up along the edge of the city and half a dozen captured T-34 tanks that had been reconditioned in the factories formed a "Beute-Panzer-Kompanie". The Russians were maintaining their pressure in the north and north-east where the "Das Reich" was having great difficulty in maintaining contact with the "GD". The SS-Panzerkorps counter-attack that Hitler so wished for remained a vain hope, especially as the "Totenkopf" was only just arriving at Poltava, some 80 Km from Kharkov. Manstein managed to wrench from the Führer the authorisation to continue with a withdrawal, whilst still hoping to retain Kharkov as an anchor for his counter-offensive, thus protecting his lines of communication towards the south-west.

The following day, on 7 February, the Germans had still not seen the columns of the 6th Cavalry Corps that were

201st Tank Brigade, in liaison with the 6th Army, to outflank the SS via the south, whilst the bulk of his Army carried on advancing.

On 6 February, the renewed assaults by Rybalko on the Donets were no more successful than the previous ones. At Skrypai, south of Chuguev, the Guards of the 62nd division, accompanied by the tanks of the 12th Corps,

This motorised German column caught in a snowstorm shows the problems faced by both sides. The weather began to improve at the end of February. (BA).

discretely advancing towards the south-west. In addition to the wintry weather consisting of strong winds, snow and short days, the other armies commanded by Golikov had monopolised the attention of the Germans. The "LAH" was still holding up Rybalko who, to Golikov's great anger, stopped his units for three days before making a new Major attempt to break through. The "Das Reich" and the "GD" were finding it increasingly difficult to hold on in the face of Kasakov's 69th Army that was gnawing away at their defences, something that Rybalko tried to exploit on his right flank. The SS division was therefore in a double vice grip around Voltchansk. The SS-AA.2 were once again called upon to extinguish the flames, with its MG-42 shattering more than one assault wave. The "Deutschland" regiment retained its advanced "jumping off" position that Hausser still hoped to use against Rybalko. Kasakov encountered more success against the "GD", a unit that was weaker and less well-equipped, north of Voltchansk. During the night, the 161st Rifle Division captured a village behind KG Kassnitz with the latter then forced to withdraw.

Once again, the situation of the Armeeabteilung deteriorated in all sectors.

"ZVEZDA" IN THE FIRMAMENT
THE BREAKTHROUGH

Despite Rybalko's setbacks on the Donets, Golikov's other armies were breaking through the German lines everywhere.

Belgorod was now clearly under threat. Despite still lacking his tank Corps and some of his infantry, Moskalenko regularly pushed back the weak 168.ID towards Belgorod. On 5 February, elements of the division were even encircled for a while at Korotcha, whilst the bulk of the 40.Armee continued its march.

Moskalenko formed an ad-hoc "mobile group" with the 183rd Rifle cut off Division and the 116th Tank Brigade in order to cut-off the town from the west, whilst the 309th Division, supported by the "M3L" and "M3M" of the 192nd Brigade approached from the north-east[20]. The reinforcements sent by Hoernlein could only assist the withdrawal of the 168.ID. KG Lorenz, formed with a Grenadier-Regiment, was held up by the road conditions and had to make do with establishing a withdrawal line south of the town. On the evening of the 7th, Moskalenko regrouped his forces that then entered into Belgorod during the night. The Germans held on until the end of the following day then withdrew in good order. Cooperation between the exhausted Landser of the 168.ID and the "Gröss-deutschland" Kampfgruppen was mediocre and the latter were left to defend the town alone, destroying as much of the infrastructure as possible. They claimed to have destroyed eight T-34 tanks, but these were more likely KV and American tanks, sometimes "brewed-up" at point blank range as they emerged from the fog. However, although the German Infantry Division

These T-34 and "M3L" were apparently seen in the streets of Belgorod, but this is a curious claim as Moskalenko's 192nd Brigade only had American tanks. In any case, the liberation of this town further weakened the German defence of Kharkov. (DR).

These Izba dwellings are typical of many Ukrainian villages that particularly suffered during the winter campaign as both sides sought to stop their respective enemy from using any form of shelter. Larger communities were often fiercely fought over. (BA).

had escaped – for now – towards the south-west, the victory was a Russian one. Moskalenko, who now at last had his remaining units, including his tank Corps, threatened the rear of the Armeeabteilung, in particular the SS-Panzerkorps, and was in a position where he could cut off Kharkov via the north.

In the south, the Cavalry, despite a certain delay encountered some success. Hausser, aware of the danger created by this gap where only a few detachments of the 298.ID and 320.ID faced the Russians, sent a KG made up of the I./SS-Pz.Rgt.1 of the "LAH" and the SS-AA.2 of the "Das Reich". He soon became held up by the bad road network south of Kharkov that even slowed down the Panzers. Although the withdrawing columns of German infantry were escaping from the pursuing Russians, the latter were trying to avoid com-

bat in order to advance around Kharkov via the south and then push on towards Merefa, 15 km south of the city, and therefore cutting off the SS-Panzerkorps. The survivors of the 298.ID still capable of fighting were made up into "Sturmbataillon 298" assault battalion 298, that was no more than an improvised KG. At the same time, the 6th Army continued its advance towards the Dobas as part of "Skachok". For the Germans, the loss of Belgorod and the increasing pressure on the z.b.V. Cramer Corps, did not give them any other option than to make a new withdrawal towards the west and Kharkov. Lanz feared that he would have to renounce his counter-attack towards the south. In the meantime, just as Hausser had wanted, the "Der Führer" regiment and the tanks of the I./SS-Pz. Rgt.2, counter-attacked Rybalko's right flank south-east

PZ IV G "221"
Kharkov, February 1943.

of Voltchansk at dawn on 9 February. The Russians, possibly of the 1st destruction division, were waiting for them. The 76.2 mm guns destroyed no less than eight German armoured vehicles and damaged several others. The SS consoled themselves by saying that they had "halted the enemy advance", which was an illusion in this case. This proved that localised attacks were not enough to stop "Zvezda" even if the advance of the Red Army was nothing like a steamroller, except for its speed. On the 10th, followed up more than pushed back by Rybalko, the SS-Panzerkorps moved to a new line of defence east of Kharkov. The battle for the city itself would now begin.

IS "ZVEZDA" STILL FADING?

After more than a week of standing still on the Donets against Armeeabteilung Lanz, Golikov appeared to have achieved the objectives of "Zvezda" thanks to Moskalenko.

Indeed, the 40th Army, now virtually at full strength, advanced on Kharkov from Belgorod, pushing back the z.b.V. Cramer Corps. In consequence, Golokov encouraged Rybalko to prevent Hausser from establishing his forces east of Kharkov. It was too late. The "LAH" and "Das Reich" held a tighter perimeter ten kilometres from the outskirts of the city. Also, Lanz could at last launch his counter-attack thanks to a withdrawal manoeuvre. It used units from both divisions to form a "Stossgruppe" – attack group – with the bulk of the "Der Führer" regiment and several units of the "LAH", including the Panzer-Regiment under the command of Dietrich, a group that was almost the size of a division[21]. At the same time, the "Das Reich" formed a "Deckungsgruppe"(cover group) to defend Kharkov from the east. The "Stossgruppe" at first aimed at hitting the 6th

Corps around Merefa whilst also recovering the remains of the 320.ID. Its "manoeuvre" began badly in the midst of a violent snow storm. Kurt Meyer, Kommandeur of SS-AA.1 stated that "the tanks pushed the mass of snow in front of them as if they were ploughs". The Tiger tanks had even more problems, slipping and pushing the piles of snow into impassable barriers, and one the tank's engines caught fire! To sum up, the German KG did not fight the Soviet Cavalry on 10-11 February, but rather the weather conditions, whilst the Guards sheltered in the woods.

Another source of worry was the fate of the 320.ID now some 20 km behind the Russian lines. This division stated on the 11th that they had more than 1,000 wounded and that the latter were sometimes forced to go on foot as there was no space in the vehicles. They moved along the east bank of the Donets and Hausser was ordered to help them cross at Zmiev. Another KG was formed around the I./SS-Pz.Gre.Rgt.1 commanded by Sturmbannführer Peiper, reinforced by a few StuG and self-propelled flak guns. Peiper had to cross two rivers, including the Donets, to bring back the 320.ID. He moved off during the night

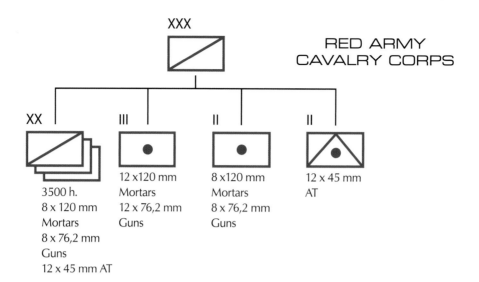

XXX

RED ARMY
CAVALRY CORPS

XX

3500 h.
8 x 120 mm
Mortars
8 x 76,2 mm
Guns
12 x 45 mm AT

III

12 x120 mm
Mortars
12 x 76,2 mm
Guns

II

8 x120 mm
Mortars
8 x 76,2 mm
Guns

II

12 x 45 mm
AT

Notes : 1. This is a theoretical organisation chart. 16,000 men approximately with 250 guns and mortars and around 16,000 horses.

2. All of the support units were not always present. The 6th Guards Cavalry Corps only had two divisions but was at full strength from 1 February onwards.

The PzKpfw III remained the mainstay of the Panzerdivisionen, even in those within the SS-Panzerkorps, forming nearly 80 % of the tank strength of the "Das Reich" and the "Totenkopf". The tank seen here belonged to a Heer division. (BA).

of 11 February, crossing the lines of the 6th Cavalry Corps and covering more than 30 km. The KG captured bridges without any difficulties or losses from the riflemen of the 350th Division. Towards 12.30 he came into contact with the 320.ID near Zmiev but had to wait until 13 February and the arrival of its rearguard 585.Grenadier-Regiment, before the division was gathered together. Naturally, the Russians made the most of this delay to recapture the bridges. The horse-drawn column of the 320. ID, escorted by KG Peiper, headed for Krassnya Polyana. The village was defended by a ski battalion that was wiped out by the SS, but not before partially blowing up the bridge. The latter was able to bear the weight of carts, but not tanks. A StuG tried to cross the ice, but the latter gave wayShowing audacity, Peiper went back the way he had come, crossed the Donets at Zmiev and followed the river behind the 6th Army, reaching Merefa in the morning whilst the 320. ID made its way directly to the German lines[22].

At the same time, the "Stossgruppe" and the 6th Cavalry Corps at last came to blows, much to the dismay of the latter which, cut-off, halted its advance. However, on the 11th, the first German assault south of Merefa resulted in a fiasco when several Panzers advanced into a marsh. Although only one remained bogged down in the mire, two others were knocked out by Russian fire. On the 12th, the 8th Cavalry Division fell back at Novaja Vologada against the "Das Reich" reconnaissance group, supported by the PzKpfw IV of the "LAH". On the right flank, the start of the SS attack was just as bad when a lack of fuel brought Meyer's group to a halt. On the left, the

Panzergrenadiere of the "LAH" were no more successful against the Cavalrymen defending Bereka. The Waffen-SS were up against veterans supported by many light artillery pieces. However, by the next day, the Germans had pushed the Guards out of Novaja Vologada and the bulk of the Corps withdrew towards the south-east accompanied by the tanks of the 201st Brigade. The T-34 tanks, with their wide tracks, encountered fewer problems moving over the terrain than the Panzers, despite the Winterketten of the latter (wider tracks with studs). The SS claimed to have destroyed the Corps, a claim that was very optimistic. Nevertheless, Lanz hoped to achieve this objective no later than 14 February.

Indeed, it was obvious in other sectors that Rybalko was not encountering any success. Between 12-14 February, he became stuck at the shortened perimeter around Kharkov held by Hausser's "Deckungsgruppe". The 3rd tank Army was badly coordinated, lacking support and its artillery was not following up, sometimes due to a lack of shells. The same applied in the air, with the Soviet air forces using make-shift or distant airfields, a problem that did not affect the Luftwaffe. On the 12th, at Rogan, 15 km from the centre of Kharkov, the 12th tank Corps and the Guards of the 62nd division broke through part of the line held by SS-Pz.Gre.Rgt.1. Reacting with their usual speed, the Germans sent two companies of SS-Pz.Gre.Rgt.2 to block any immediate breakthrough. Nevertheless, the Russians reinforced the ground taken and their mortars laid down a heavy barrage onto the SS, thus preventing a probable counter-attack.

These Sdkfz 251 were of precious help within the Panzerdivisionen as they could, in General, rely on a battalion of motorised infantry, at least within the SS-Panzerkorps. The "GD" did not have such troops. (BA).

22 - *Peiper was decorated with the Ritterkreuz on 9 March for this exploit.*

Less mobile than their adversary, the Frontoviki could, however, rely on good winter equipment. The weapon seen here is a DP light machine-gun. (DR).

Three German armoured vehicles, from left to right a Sdkfz 222, Sdkfz 260 and Sdkfz 221 seem to be posing for the photo. These vehicles equipped, amongst others, the "GD" reconnaissance group that plotted the Soviet advance towards Kharkov. (BA).

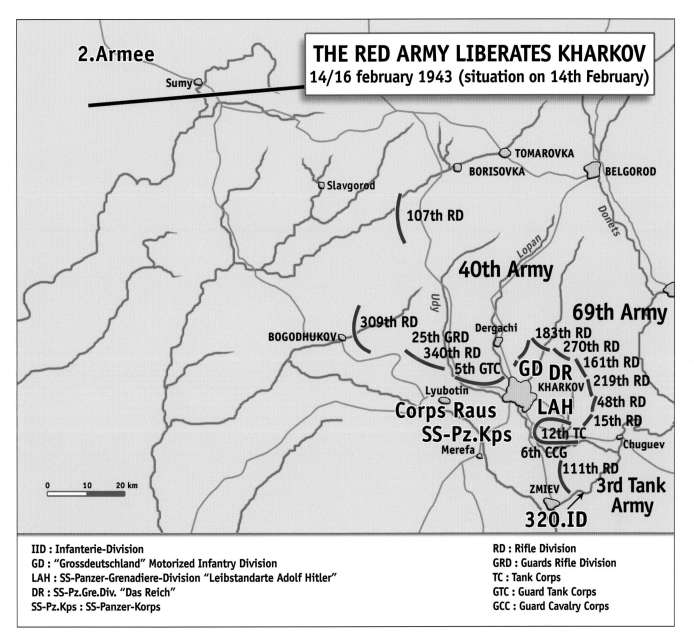

THE RED ARMY LIBERATES KHARKOV
14/16 february 1943 (situation on 14th February)

2.Armee

Sumy

TOMAROVKA
BORISOVKA
BELGOROD

Slavgorod

Donets

Lopan

107th RD

40th Army

Udy

69th Army

309th RD
BOGODHUKOV

25th GRD
340th RD
5th GTC

Dergachi

183th RD
270th RD
161th RD
219th RD
48th RD
15th RD

GD DR
KHARKOV
LAH

Lyubotin

Corps Raus
SS-Pz.Kps

12th TC

Merefa

6th CCG

Chuguev

111th RD

ZMIEV

3rd Tank
Army

320.ID

0   10   20 km

IID : Infanterie-Division
GD : "Grossdeutschland" Motorized Infantry Division
LAH : SS-Panzer-Grenadiere-Division "Leibstandarte Adolf Hitler"
DR : SS-Pz.Gre.Div. "Das Reich"
SS-Pz.Kps : SS-Panzer-Korps

RD : Rifle Division
GRD : Guards Rifle Division
TC : Tank Corps
GTC : Guard Tank Corps
GCC : Guard Cavalry Corps

It was not until nightfall that, under intensive German artillery fire, the T-70, T-34 and Frontoviks pushed the last Panzergrenadiere out of the ruins of the town. In the south, the assaults of the 111th division resulted in bloody failures and the SS withdrew to a new line. However, although Hausser's men were withdrawing, they were exhausting Rybalko's forces before they could enter into Kharkov. Also, the "Totenkopf" arrived in Poltava beginning on 11 February, followed the next day by the first Panzers. Finally, north-east of Kharkov, facing the "GD" and the "Das Reich", the 69th Army advanced at a rate that was just as slow as the 3rd tank Army with whom they had at least made a solid link. The "GD" was just as prompt as the SS when dealing with any crisis.

On the 10th, a gap opened up with the "Das Reich", forming a breach in the defences. The Kommandeur of the Pioniere-Bataillon gathered together a handful of his men, 50 artillerymen without their guns and two PaK guns, and with this improvised Kampfgruppe, halted in-extremis the riflemen of the 180th division before the intervention of the FBB. Kasakov resigned himself to slowly push back the Germans with his weakened divisions, lacking artillery and tank support. In the light of these conditions, capturing Kharkov was going to be a tough nut to crack.

As for Hitler, he continued pressuring Lang to hold on to Kharkov whatever the cost, and Lang's Armeeab-teilung was placed under the direct orders of Manstein,

Kharkov was a major railhead and armoured trains such as the one seen here were used to protect the line, installations, supply trains and equipment. (BA).

23 - *Rostov was liberated on 14 February.*
24 - *On 10 February, Cramer was replaced by General der Panzertruppen Raus.*
25 - *The 4th Corps received the title of Guards due to having closed the encirclement of Stalingrad by joining together the prongs of the 13th mechanised Corps to the south-east of the city.*

whose HG Sud "absorbed" HG "B". However, the situation was worsening all around the Ukrainian city. Indeed, although the 6th Army was not advancing rapidly, it was still moving towards the west, slowed down more by the weather than the Germans, and its advanced parties were already south-west of Kharkov, a short distance from Krasnograd. Vatutin was ordered to reach the Dnieper, a task of the utmost importance that was initially given to the Popov group. The Stavka and Stalin remained optimistic as the "fascists" were withdrawing south of Kursk, and Golikov appeared to be on the point of liberating Kharkov, despite the presence of the SS who were probably tasked with covering the withdrawal[23].

At that precise time, the main threat to Lanz was Moskalenko's 40th Army. After having completed the capture of Belgorod on 9 February, the Soviet General sent forward his troops once more the following day towards the south. He met with immediate success, encircling a battalion of Grenadier-Regiment "GD", commanded by Hauptmann Remer, who managed to force open a gap towards Kharkov thanks to a few Panzers. Moskalenko planned to gradually push back the Raus Corps towards the south whilst at the same time encircling it via the west with his 5th Guards Tank Corps[24]. Although this was not a fresh unit, like the SS-Pz.Gre.Div., it gave Moskalenko a veritable mobile group to fight against the enemy lines that were still spread very

thin. Also, the 5th Corps was commanded by an excellent officer, General Kravchenko, who was capable of exploiting the slightest gap and who, unlike his fellow officers of the 3rd tank Army, avoided vain frontal attacks[25]. These cracks in the line appeared on 12 February at Dergatchi, a small town defended by the A.A. "GD". About to be cut off by Kravchenko's Brigades, the reconnaissance group preferred to withdraw. Lanz was furious and ordered that the village be immediately retaken. Hoernlein sent reinforcements – the FBB, III./Gre.Rgt. "GD", the PaK of the "Das Reich" and a few Panzers of which there were only nine available. These weak "battalions" initially forced out Kravchenko's riflemen, but by nightfall, the arrival of the 25th division Guards forced the Germans to definitively give up Dergatchi. The A.A. "GD" contented itself with keeping an eye on the advance of the 5th Corps which was slipping towards the south-west, whilst Moskalenko's riflemen followed the exhausted elements of the 168. ID. Golikov then ordered the commander of the 40th Army to take Kharkov by the 13th at the latest before continuing towards the west. By the evening of 13 February, the Soviet infantry had established a foothold in the interior defensive perimeter, whilst Kravchenko's tanks gradually cut-off the city via the north-west. The Germans still held on, but their situation looked to be hopeless.

"Zvezda" appeared to be on the verge of success.

REFUSING TO CARRY OUT ORDERS

On 14 February 1943, Armeeabteilung Lanz was in an extremely exposed position. Despite the tactical successes of Hitler's Praetorian Guard, the bulk of the SS-Panzerkorps was at risk of being encircled at Kharkov, raising the spectre of a second Stalingrad despite the approaching "Totenkopf". Whilst Kazakov and Rybalko slowly and with difficulty squeezed the "LAH" and the "Das Reich", Moskalenko placed the lid on the box. By the end of the day, the riflemen of the 340th division and the M3L and M3M of the 192nd Brigade entered into the northern suburbs of Kharkov whilst Kravchenko, despite the mobile screen of the "GD" light tanks, slipped towards the west, cutting off the railway and Lioubotin. The Germans only held a narrow corridor of less than ten kilometres in width towards the south-east and Poltava. Hausser knew that he did not have the means to defend Kharkov despite Hitler's exhortations to the contrary, which the latter stated once more in a message received at dawn[26]. The 213.Sich.Div. had under its command the remains of its police regiments and a few hastily assembled Alarmenheinten – "alarm detachments". Almost all of the fighting troops were on the perimeter with the "GD" under Raus's command in the north, the Waffen-SS in the north-east and east, along with the weak 320. ID.

Hausser read the increasingly worrying reports throughout 14 February. Although his "Angriffsgruppe" was holding off the 3rd tank Army and his "Deckungsgruppe" was fulfilling its covering role, Moskalenko's men had begun to lay siege to the city, breaking through an area between the 168. ID, pushed back to the west, and the "GD".

During this time, the 6th Army was less than 30 km south of Kharkov and was marching towards the Dnieper, threatening Krasnograd and Poltava. In other words, the garrison was at risk of being caught in a trap and wiped out. When the commander of the SS-Panzerkorps was informed by the 213.Sich.Div. that "civilians" were shooting at German soldiers in Kharkov, he gave his first orders for the evacuation of the city[27]. Hausser, an early member of the SS, remained a competent officer and knew, as did Lanz and Manstein, that Kharkov could not be defended in the present situation. Hitler, totally traumatised by Stalingrad, refused the idea of a new defeat, even if Kharkov did not have the same symbolic value as Stalingrad. The dictator, however, remained loyal to his old demons and ordered the city to be held! Lanz, upon hearing of the preparations to evacuate the city, twice repeated the order to hold the city, the second time directly by telephone. The SS officer replied that he would "hold Kharkov to the last man", which was starting to look as if it would be the case.

At Kharkov and elsewhere, Flak played an essential role in the defence of the city. The 88 guns were relatively mobile weapons due to their well-designed mounts. (BA).

26 - The message simply stated that "Kharkov must be held to the last man".

27 - The threat of a hypothetical "uprising" in a city stripped of its population was used by Hausser as a justification as there were hardly any partisans in Kharkov.

Although it suffered from the fighting, Kharkov was already a city devastated by the war and the occupation, as seen in this German photograph taken at the beginning of 1943. (BA).

Indeed, by 14 February the encirclement was almost complete. Golikov, whose star had seemed to be fading over the last 24 hours, ordered a General assault in the light of the spectacular progress made by Moskalenko and Kravchenko. Although he could not count upon a "fifth column" within the city, despite the fears of Hausser, his forces now encircled the defenders. The 40th Army was to enter Kharkov by the north and west, the 69th Army by the north-west and the 3rd Tank Army by the east and south.

The fatigue and losses of the last weeks against an adversary tougher than the Italians and Hungarians was starting to tell and the commissars pushed the Frontoviki to take from the fascists another large city, and one which was more important than Stalingrad. However, the fighting remained fierce everywhere.

The Angriffsgruppe continued in its attempt to destroy the 6th Cavalry Corps that was trying to keep open a corridor towards the west around Bereka in order to withdraw. To achieve this, the Russians wanted to push the AA and "LAH" out of Alexeyevka. Using a snow storm as cover, the riflemen infiltrated the weakly held German lines before being pushed back by a counter-attack formed by SS light tanks. With supplies running low, a small column of half-tracks and Panzers carrying fuel and shells pushed through and arrived

just in time to hold off a fresh attack. But, although the SS saved Kurt Meyer's reconnaissance group, they were halted in front of Bereka where the 201st Tank Brigade held the narrow corridor through which the Cavalry escaped. Although it failed in its attempt to cut off Kharkov from the south, the 6th Corps had at least survived the German counter-attack and could now lean against Golikov's other armies. The remains of the 320. ID were then formed into a reserve due to the multiple threats. In the east, the "Deckungsruppe" was having a hard time holding off the Frontoviki of Rybalko and Kazakov. In the south-east, coming from Chuguev, the 62nd Guards division and the tanks of the 179th Brigade gradually pushed back the elements of the "LAH". Moskalenko arrived at the same time from the west and the A.A. "GD" was unable to hold off Kravchenko's tanks that entered the suburbs of Kharkov. Hoernlein had to scrape the bottom of the barrel to form a defensive line. The next day, the commander of the 40th Army sent into action the riflemen of the 340th division and the 25th Guards division to accompany Kravenchenko's T-34 and T-70 tanks. They came up against the elements of the "GD" that were defending the access to the city centre. At Lioubotin, south-west of Kharkov, the Russians surprised a column heading west and destroyed 50 vehicles, losses

that were admitted by the Germans themselves! This was part of the Fusilier-Regiment that had hastily deployed before receiving the support of the divisional StuG-Abt. that had just been issued with 20 brand new vehicles unloaded the previous day at Kharkov station. They destroyed the few tanks present and dispersed the riflemen, thus opening once more the route towards the east. The Russians did not immediately realise it, but the Germans were evacuating the city. Hausser, torn between his duty to obey orders and a more objective analysis of the situation, had made his decision. His divisions, weakened and physically worn out by two weeks of intense Russian winter warfare, could not hold out for long once the city was cut off. This was particularly true for the Heer units, including the "GD". Its infantry was exhausted and decimated and the delivery of the Sturmgeschütze was an exceptional event given the division's materiel situation. The SS-Panzer-Grenadiere-Divisionen, despite being in better condition, also felt the effects of the battle. Although the "LAH" could field almost two-thirds of its armour with a strong infantry force, the same did not apply to the "Das Reich". Indeed, the latter only had 21 operational Panzers and 18 StuG, whereas at the end of January, it had 131 and 31 respectively. The six captured KV-1 and T-34 now used against their former owners were

no more than a stop-gap solution. Note that at this stage of the battle, the powerful Tiger tanks of the two divisions were not very efficient due to the crew's lack of experience. Finally, the "Totenkopf" had still not arrived. Elements of the latter that were due to arrive in Kiev took four days to reach Poltava when a sudden thaw turned the snow into a sea of mud! The most advanced units reached Krasnograd and at least covered Hausser's rear.

To sum up, upon learning at 13.00 hrs on 15 February that the first Soviet units had entered into Kharkov, in particular those of Moskalenko, who threatened his rear and supply lines, the SS-Panzerkorps commander gave the order to abandon the city. The escape corridor quickly narrowed to a few kilometres and Hausser knew that the "GD" would not be able to hold off the enemy advance. Lanz, in agreement with Manstein, deemed that the right decision had been made, contrary to those of Hitler who the same morning, repeated his order to hold the city. Hausser reported Kharkov's abandon without waiting for his superiors to reply in order to present them, and Hitler of course, with the fait accompli. He also informed Raus of his decision[28].

The Germans began their withdrawal at the end of the afternoon.

On 14 February, Soviet tanks and infantrymen entered into Kharkov but came up against a ferocious defence, even though the vice seemed to be tightening against the defenders.
(DR).

28 - *It would appear that the order was sent to the "GD" with some delay.*

35

This PaK 38 anti-tank gun appears to be waiting for a target. Generally speaking, the Germans managed to keep the Russians at arm's length and were thus able to withdraw, albeit with some difficulty, towards the west. (BA).

This photograph of a StuG belonging to an unidentified unit highlights the low profile of this armoured vehicle. It took a heavy toll of Russian armour, such as on 15 February when the decisive intervention of the "GD" Sturmgeschütze managed to keep open a corridor for the withdrawal of the SS-Panzerkorps. (BA).

RETREAT FROM RUSSIA

In the city itself, despite the lack of any partisan assistance, the Frontoviki continued to apply pressure. Nevertheless, the departure of the SS-Panzerkorps and the 231.Sich.Div. was carried out in good order. Units in position in the east began withdrawing slowly at 17.00 hrs, allowing the engineers to sabotage or booby trap several depots and bridges. They did not manage to destroy many large buildings, however, something that underlines the haste in which the SS-Panzerkorps left the city. The bulk of the forces had to withdraw from Kharkov before nightfall and the 320. ID moved to the west and south-west of the city, on the river Udy, to help the withdrawal of the SS and the "GD".

The "Das Reich" "Deustchland" regiment provided the bulk of the covering force in front of Kazakov and Rybalko and, with the efficient support of the division's PaK and StuG, pulled off a brilliant rearguard action. The tanks of the SS-Pz.Rgt.2 formed an ambush against the leading units of the 15th Corps and destroyed 15 armoured vehicles. However, by the evening of the 15th, most of the city was in Soviet hands and they saw the German movements as being new proof of a

A German automobile column advances with difficulty over a Russian road. The evacuation of Kharkov was undertaken in good order, but the Soviets captured many of the supply depots. (BA).

This "Leibstandarte" PzKpfw IV was supposedly damaged during the first battle of Kharkov but was perhaps recovered by the Germans? (BA).

Two views of T-34 tanks belonging to a unit of Rybalko's 3rd tank Army entering into Kharkov. Note the large buildings. (DR).

withdrawal to the Dnieper and therefore began preparations to pursue the Germans. In Kharkov, the fighting continued throughout the night, lit up by the fires started by the Germans or resulting from bombardments. In the north, the riflemen of the 183rd Division infiltra-

ted the lines held by the "GD" and took by surprise the Pioniere laying explosive charges. Hoernlein and his officers resorted to amazing improvisation and initiative in order to form small reserve forces along the axis of withdrawal and at dawn on 16 February, almost all of the garrison had withdrawn, and set up a more or less coherent defence line against the Voronej Front.

Hausser's refusal to obey orders caused an immediate stir within the General staffs. Five minutes after having ordered the withdrawal, the SS-Panzerkorps commander informed Lanz of his decision, stating the flimsiness of the defensive perimeter and once more, the "partisan" activity within Kharkov. Lanz therefore flew to meet him in a Fieseler Storch and give him a sharp talking to. Upon learning this, Manstein thought it better to talk with Lanz before either taking disciplinary action against Hausser or approving his decision, and therefore no counter-order was sent to the SS-Panzerkorps. Although Hausser's two direct superior officers approved a decision that saved the spearhead of a counter-offensive, naturally Hitler did not see things in the same light and saw this, quite rightly, as a refusal to carry out one of his direct orders.

The Germans evacuated the city in good order and formed a defensive line to the west. These infantrymen are setting up a MG 34 on a heavy mount. Hausser's SS troops used the even more formidable MG 42. (BA).

On the 17th, he arrived on his personal Focke-Wulf Condor at Manstein's headquarters at Zaporoje on the Dnieper. The aircraft was escorted by fighters, but the danger came from the ground. Indeed, the tanks of the 25th Corps, the 6th Army's mobile group, had reached Pavlograd, a mere 50 km from Mansteins' HQ, and there were no German fighting units between the two towns[29]. However, Manstein did not deem the situation hopeless, on the contrary, as the SS-Panzerkorps was now out of the Kharkov trap, and he explained his point of view to Hitler. The latter, in a state of fury due to the loss of the Ukrainian city and who had no doubt flown to Manstein's HQ in order to remove the head of HG Sud from his command, ended up being convinced. Also, with these two offensives, the Red Army had seen its supply problems reach a critical point. Manstein therefore considered that it was time to react and recapture Kharkov. Hitler demanded that the city be the main objective, whereas Manstein wanted to first eliminate the forces lining the Dnieper, including the Popov group. The delay of the "Totenkopf", still partly stuck in the mud, and Manstein's explanations, convinced Hitler to accept the plan and not sack the

commander. The critical circumstances and the possibility of a huge victory that would make up in some way for the series of disasters that had struck the Germans since November, explain Hitler's leniency.

Although he did not like Manstein, the latter had presented an audacious plan in 1940 that had led to the defeat of the French Army, then two years later, his last great victory in the USSR, taking Sebastopol in July 1942 after having inflicted a crushing defeat against the Russian armies in the Crimea[30]. The thought of his elite guard taking part in the offensive also reassured Hitler. Although the head of HG Sud did not obtain sole command of the Ostheer as he had wished for, he was allowed to plan his offensive in the way that he saw fit.

The atmosphere in the Soviet camp was totally different. In the Kremlin, Stalin was jubilant when he heard that Kharkov had been liberated and a feel-ing of optimism took over the Stavka despite a few voices that doubted the collapse of the German Army. Golikov was already planning his armies' movements towards the Dnieper and pushed that of Rybalko to the south of the city. In Kharkov itself, the fighting caused

29 - *Pavlograd was initially defended by the "Colonna Carloni", an Italian detachment formed around elements of the 6th Bersaglieri, the last Italian combatant unit engaged in the USSR. It remained stuck in this town due to a lack of petrol!*

30 - *Also, in Crimea, Manstein made sure that his troops collaborated with zeal with the Einsatzgruppe D, initially in the murder of the Jewish community in the peninsula.*

A Bf 109 and a Fw58 multi-role aircraft at an airfield. The Soviet advance led to a decrease in air support as the latter suffered from logistical problems when the Luftwaffe operated from well-equipped bases. (BA).

some confusion within the ranks of Moskalenko and Kasakov's armies. Kravchenko's tanks and Rybalko's riflemen linked up in Sverdlov Street around 10 o'clock on 16 February. The soldiers' joy was soon shared by some of the last inhabitants of Kharkov. The population hardly reached 200,000, barely 25% of that of June 1941. Luckily, the Germans had not had enough time

to carry out their usual destruction, and several of their depots were used to make up for the lack of civilian and military supplies. Although the stocks of "liberated" alcohol did not apparently cause any major problems, several columns soon found themselves stuck or mixed up with others, and the arrival of the 3rd Tank Armies supply trains made the log jam even worse. It took

slightly apprehensive at the return of Stalin's regime, they did not regret the depart of the "master race". The population hoped for a better future, especially in the light of the fighting that was moving westwards. The liberation of Kharkov boosted the morale of his men, but Golikov, like other Generals, was worried, despite the apparent victory. "Zvezda", as planned, had led to the liberation of Kharkov, but had not wiped out the enemy forces. On the contrary, the wear and tear and state of exhaustion of the Soviet forces had become a source of worry. The Rifle Divisions fielded less than 65% of their nominal strength at the beginning of the month. Those of Moskalenko now had 3,500 to 4,000 men and those of Kazakov, wiped out by frontally pushing back the "Das Reich", sometimes had 1,000[32]. As for the armaments, some divisional artillery regiments had barely twenty guns instead of the usual 32. Golikov had asked for 19,000 personnel, but had only received 1,600 since the beginning of "Zvezda". Civilians, recruited more or less voluntarily around Kharkov, only partially made up for the loss of veterans[33]. For the mobile forces, Rybalko's 3rd Army was down to 100, a total increased to 110 a few days later. Despite being at 75% strength, the 6th Cavalry Corps was still lacking in punch, and the 201st Brigade that was attached to it was reduced to a large tank company. The few captured and re-used German Panzers and guns were a drop in the ocean compared to what it was lacking.

Despite the success of "Zvezda", Golikov knew that he would come across the German mechanised units along a new line of defence.

"Na zapad!" – "to the west!"

31 - *The Soviets left behind measures such as these in 1941 when evacuating several cities like Kiev.*

32 - *It should be remembered that a Rifle Division had a theoretical strength of almost 9,400 men.*

33 - *The "partisans" encountered by the Germans were often recruits such as these, rarely clothed from head to foot in regulation uniform.*

T-34 tanks of a non-identified Voronezh Front unit roll down the Sverdlov road in Kharkov as they cross the city in order to push Hausser's men towards the west. Many hoped that this new victory really heralded the defeat and the withdrawal of the German Army in Russia. (DR).

three days for the traffic problem to be sorted out! This goes to show that the Red Army was still lacking experience at that time in managing its mechanised units. However, Golikov sent special NKVD bomb disposal teams to remove the booby traps and time delay bombs left behind by the Germans, and the city was not devastated[31]. Although some people were

THE REICH STRIKES BACK

Another view of a T-34 of the 3rd Tank Army in Kharkov. Rybalko's men were no longer able to attack, but the Stavka thought that the Germans were retreating.
(DR)

Feldmarschall Manstein, Commander of HG Süd. (DR)

By mid-February 1943, the fortunes of war were still smiling for the Red Army that had liberated Kharkov, the second largest city in the Ukraine, whereas the Reich and its allies appeared to be in full retreat. Two weeks after the surrender of the 6.Armee at Stalingrad, the Russians had gone from success to success in a campaign that had started in November 1942. Stalin made the most of this to proclaim himself Marshal of the Soviet Union. However, the situation in the Donbas was about to change in the most spectacular fashion. Although Golikov had liberated Kharkov, Hausser, Raus and Lanz still presented a continuous front line whilst Manstein added the finishing touches to his strategy that would hit the Voronej and south-west Fronts. Abandoning Kharkov had allowed him to retain his "fist", the SS-Panzerkorps, a force now at full strength, plus a few reinforcements such as the 15. ID that had arrived from France. Despite all this the situation did not look good for Manstein as the 6th army was advancing towards

his headquarters behind the 25th Tank Corps. On 19 February, the 111th Tank Brigade reached Slavgorod, only 30 km from Zaporoje, but the commander of HG Sud, his command confirmed by Hitler, took the risk. By relinquishing ground he was letting the Soviet armies, weakened and far from their supply depots, enter the trap that he was setting with General Hoth's 4.Panzer-Armee. The latter, an expert in tank warfare, received the SS-Panzerkorps and the XLVIII. Pz.Kps with two under-strength Panzerdivisionen. Hausser positioned himself behind Armeeabteilung Lanz, which retained the Raus Corps along with the "LAH", "GD" and a "Totenkopf" regiment to halt Golikov. In the south, the other German armies held their positions or, like the XL.Pz.Kps of the 1.Panzer-Armee, hit the Popov group. Hoth's two Corps would have to take the over-stretched 6th army in a pincer movement, then head north-east, joined by the XL.Pz.Kps. At dawn on 19 February, the first elements of the 15. ID arrived in-extremis at the Sinelkovo rail station, east of the Dnieper. The Landser pushed

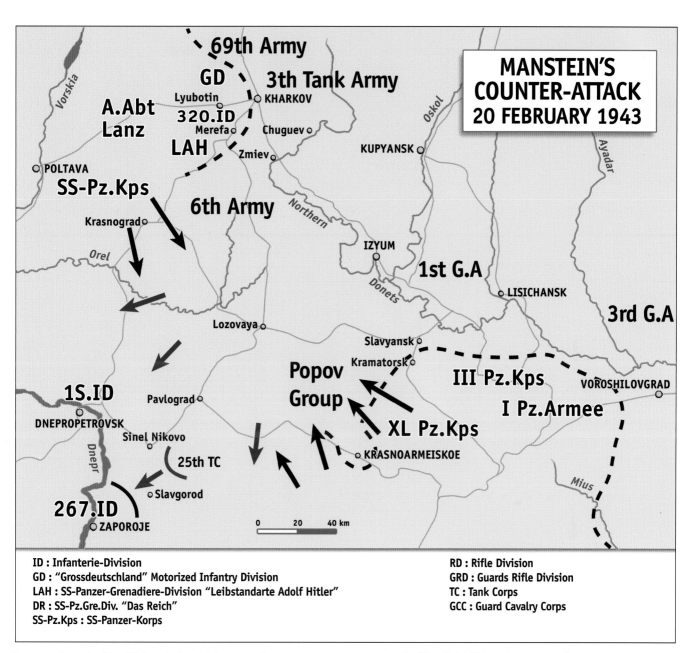

MANSTEIN'S COUNTER-ATTACK 20 FEBRUARY 1943

69th Army

GD
3th Tank Army

A.Abt
Lanz

Lyubotin
320.ID

KHARKOV

Merefa
Chuguev

LAH

Zmiev

KUPYANSK

POLTAVA

SS-Pz.Kps

6th Army

Northern

Krasnograd

Orel

IZYUM

1st G.A

LISICHANSK

Donets

3rd G.A

Lozovaya

Slavyansk

Popov
Group

Kramatorsk

III Pz.Kps

VOROSHILOVGRAD

1S.ID

Pavlograd

XL Pz.Kps

I Pz.Armee

DNEPROPETROVSK

Sinel Nikovo

KRASNOARMEISKOE

Mius

25th TC

Dnepr

Slavgorod

267.ID

ZAPOROJE

0   20   40 km

ID : Infanterie-Division
GD : "Grossdeutschland" Motorized Infantry Division
LAH : SS-Panzer-Grenadiere-Division "Leibstandarte Adolf Hitler"
DR : SS-Pz.Gre.Div. "Das Reich"
SS-Pz.Kps : SS-Panzer-Korps

RD : Rifle Division
GRD : Guards Rifle Division
TC : Tank Corps
GCC : Guard Cavalry Corps

back the Guards of the 35th and 41st divisions, caught by surprise by this audacious move. A few heavy PaK kept the Russian tanks at arm's length and removed any immediate danger to Zaporoje and Dniepropetrovsk. The counter-attack could now begin.

MANSTEIN'S MOVE

Manstein first targeted Vatutin's two spearhead armies, the 6th Army commanded by General Kharitonov and the Popov group, along the Dnieper.
At dawn on an ice cold and foggy 20 February 1943, the sky fell in on the 6th army. Out of Poltava and Kras-

nograd came not only the "Das Reich" Kampfgruppen with almost 60 Panzers and StuG, charging against the 6th Division, but also, as soon as the sun broke through, the Stukas of Luftflotte 4, also attacking the neighbouring divisions. Thanks to the proximity of the airfields to the front line, the Luftwaffe achieved air superiority during the counter-offensive, carrying out an average number of sorties three times higher than that of the Soviets that were flying from airstrips that were too distant or rudimentary. These attacks did not change Vatutin's optimism who insisted on reaching the Dnieper whatever the cost, and his Tank Corps were still heading in that direction. But, on 21 February, the "Totenkopf" at last

A German solider in a Sdkfz 251 looks across the snowy plains. Manstein's counter-offensive allowed the large German mechanised units to make full use of their tactical flexibility. *(BA).*

Whilst the German armoured divisions struck, the infantry was still faced with the Soviet assaults, particularly to the west of Kharkov. The anti-tank defence relied mainly on towed guns such as this 5 cm PaK 38. *(BA).*

reached the "Das Reich" following a difficult approach that cost it six Panzers lost to accidents! The 6th army then came under attack by two divisions that cut up its northern flank. It then hastily covered Pavlograd where it had its forward depots, with the 35th Guards division and the tanks of the 1st Guards Corps, hit on the 22nd by the "Das Reich"[1]. The same day, Vatutin ordered Kharitonov, whose 6th army was in shreds, to continue advancing with his mobile group, reinforced by the 1st Corps! The 25th Tank Corps took Slavgorod only to find itself cut off and without supplies, one hundred kilometres ahead of the army! Threatened in the north-east by the "Das Reich" and in the south-east by the 6.Panzer-Division, it escaped the next day by abandoning most of its materiel. The "Totenkopf" then attacked north of Pavlograd with some 90 Panzers, including nine Tigers, but stalled in the face of enemy positions that included T-34 tanks buried up to their turrets. This

minor failure meant that at that time the link was broken between the two SS divisions. However, Vatutin's optimism could no longer escape the truth, especially when the XLVIII.Pz.Kps also advanced from the south. Despite this, he redeployed his reinforcements and asked for assistance from the Voronej Front, believing that he was only dealing with a limited counter-attack protecting the German retreat! On 24 February, the two SS divisions at last took Pavlograd and linked up. Fearing friendly fire due to the fact that both sides were using white winter camouflage, the "Das Reich" radios sent messages identifying themselves and saying "Don't fire!", to which a "Totenkopf" radio operator replied "We only fire on worthwhile targets".

The 6th Army therefore retreated in confusion and in the evening, the 41st Guards division approaching from the south-west, reached Pavlograd, following an order received the previous day. Having recovered from the

1 - *The 1st Guards Tank Corps, one of the rare fresh units sent to reinforce Vatutin and Golikov, arrived within the 6th army on 19 February with 150 T-70 and T-34.*

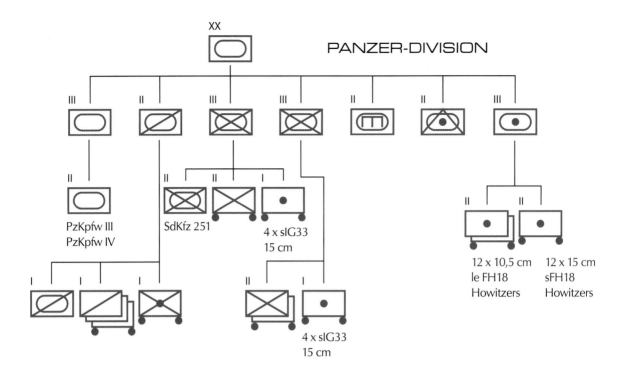

PANZER-DIVISION

XX

III — II — III — III — II — II — III

II

PzKpfw III
PzKpfw IV

II — II — I

SdKfz 251

4 x sIG33
15 cm

II — II

12 x 10,5 cm
le FH18
Howitzers

12 x 15 cm
sFH18
Howitzers

I — I — I

II — I

4 x sIG33
15 cm

Notes : *This is a VERY theoretical organisation chart.*
No German armoured division was at full strength and they rarely had more than fifty tanks....
The same applies to support units. Several divisions did not have mechanised battalions equipped with Sdkfz 251 and most of the anti-tank weapons were towed. The 4.Pz.Div. of the 2.Armee used its Marder II within its Panzer-Regiment due to a lack of PzKpfw IV.

Manstein's counter-offensive inflicted heavy losses against the Soviet forces, as seen here with these wrecks, one of which is a T-34. *(BA).*

Panzers of a Heer division pass by a 15 cm sIG 33 howitzer used by artillery companies of infantry regiments and Panzergrenadiere. The drawback with this gun was its heavy weight that affected its towing capabilities. (BA).

initial surprise, it withdrew from the trap using the cover of darkness and headed towards the north-east, but almost all of the divisional staff were caught. Squeezed on all sides, the 6th army now found itself in full retreat. By the 23rd, Manstein no longer saw Kharitonov as a threat.

As for the Popov group, whose action largely fell outside the scope of the battle for Kharkov, its destruction was tasked to the decimated divisions of the 1.Panzer-Armee. With four Tank Corps, three Rifle Divisions, (two of which were Guards), two tank and three ski Brigades, this armoured army never had its full complement of 700 tanks. On 19 February, one of its best units, the 4th Guards Tank Corps, escaped decimated from an encirclement at Krasnoarmeskoye. Still, with its 35 T-34 and 15 T-70, it was in better shape than the 10th Corps with its 17 tanks. The fol-lowing day, poor Popov, who had requested to withdraw his weak and exhausted units to a more defendable line, was ordered by Vatutin to carry on pushing forward. The Stavka reproached the

General Vatutin, commander of the South-West Front, continued in his belief that the Germans were in full retreat when Manstein launched his counter-offensive. Although he was a good officer and strategist, he was let down on several occasions by his excessive optimism. (BA).

Although Soviet tank Corps and Brigades always used nearly 40% of light tanks, the PzKpfw III "kurz" was still used by the Heer Panzerdivisionen. The tank seen here is in a shelter to conceal it from enemy aircraft. (BA).

A StuG and a Sdkfz 252 ammunition supply vehicle of StuG-Lehr Batterie.901 that fought alongside the 19.Pz.Div. of the XL.Pz.Kps during Manstein's counter-offensive. (BA).

Two Soviet riflemen in winter clothing, February 1943.

commander of the mobile group for his "delays" and lack of "action"!

The Krasnoarmeskoye "pocket" was the beginning of the Manstein offensive. Between 21 and 24 February, the 7.Pz.Div., 11.Pz.Div. and SS-Div. "Wiking" tore the dispersed and vulnerable Popov group into pieces. The XL.Pz.Kps linked up with the XLVIII. Pz.Kps on its left flank and on the 25th, a veritable armoured finger chased towards the north the remains of the Popov group, the 6th army and elements of the 1st Guards army that was hardly any better off. Vatutin at last realised the magnitude of the German reaction and called the Stavka for help whilst Manstein prepared to launch the next phase of his offensive. In one week, his forces had destroyed or captured 180 tanks and 370 guns, eliminating more than 15,000 Frontoviki. This radical change in the situation was also thanks to the fierce resistance put up by Armee-Abteilung Kempf in front of the Voronej Front.

Whilst his 6th army was being battered, Golikov continued his offensive to the west of Kharkov.

GOLIKOV VS KEMPF

The capture of Kharkov initially caused a little confusion within the ranks of the Voronej Front.

Golikov's first task was to install some order. There were three army staffs, ten Rifle Divisions and Brigades and two Tank Corps within Kharkov and its closest suburbs. Starting on the evening of 16 February, the 12th and 15th Tank Corps took on the elements of the "GD" and "Das Reich" west of the city, whilst the 48th Guards Rifle Division took the rail station at Osnovo along with important supply dumps. However, the bulk of the forces were stalled in the city centre, held up by destroyed infrastructure or just by traffic jams, especially when a brief thaw turned the snowy terrain into lakes of mud! Nevertheless, Rybalko, under the orders of Golikov, carried on with the offensive towards Poltava, the logistical base of the Germans and which, if lost, would really make them retreat to the Dnieper.

Rybalko, second from the left, talks with some of the Tankisti of his 3rd Tank Army. His troops were being worn out in vain against the defence put up by Kempf to the west of Kharkov. (DR).

The 3rd Tank Army deployed west of Kharkov, flanked on its right by the 69th army, with Moskalenko's 40th army sent towards the north in a large sweeping movement that it concluded on the 21st, facing the 168. ID. Rybalko and Kasakov confronted the Raus Corps, the tough core of Armeeabteilung Kempf. Indeed, on 19 February, Lanz had handed his command to General der Panzertruppen Kempf, an excellent officer. Lanz had led well but was used as a scapegoat for the loss of Kharkov. Hausser, the "father" of the Waffen-SS and liked by Himmler, could not be directly sanctioned, especially as his men played the main role in the counter-offensive. Armeeabteilung

Kempf was mostly made up of the 168.ID and the Raus Corps comprised of the "GD", "LAH" and a "Totenkopf" regiment. Rybalko maintained the pressure on the "GD" that was covering the west of Kharkov, flanked on its right by the 320.ID, with the "LAH" covering the south-west, thus allowing the departure of the "Das Reich" on the 17th. The following day, the 15th Tank Corps charged into two companies of the III./Gren.Rgt. "GD" who, due to a lack of PaK guns, were literally crushed by the T-34 and T-70 that dealt with the few Panzers present. At the same time in Merefa, the 320. ID were having a hard time against the 12th Corps and the 111th Division.

Il-2 Type 3, unknown unit, Ukraine, March 1943.

Another PaK, in action for the photograph given its exposed position? The German anti-tank defence remained efficient when it combined towed guns with self-propelled artillery such as the StuG or Marder. (BA).

On the 19th, the Soviet Corps by-passed the defenders only to come across the "Totenkopf" Thule regiment which, supported by an artillery group and the bulk of StuG-Abt. "Totenkopf", stopped the advance in its tracks. The previous day, another breach, the result of confusion between the 320.ID and the "LAH", was closed by a battalion of Gre. Rgt.586, some StuG and SS engineers who fought off the riflemen of the 184th division at Borki. On 20 February, Peiper and other "LAH" units chased the Russians from the railway station where they had dug in. Despite Rybalko's exhortations, his tired soldiers failed against the Raus Corps that was covering, as planned, the SS-Panzerkorps which could attack the 6th army the same day. Also, Kempf was waiting for the 167.ID, arriving from Holland[2]. All this did not

stop Golikov however. On the contrary, as when he had redeployed Moskalenko's army, he continued his offensive with his second echelon, preventing the Germans from catching their breath. Despite the arrival of the "Thule" regiment and the approach of the 167. ID, they held a thinly manned line, even if their vehicles allowed them to get from one hot spot to another. Once more, the 40th army played an important role. Despite the delay caused by its movement, on foot, on 19 February it continued its slow, methodical march against the weak 168. ID that was spread out over 60 km[3]. The division had virtually no artillery left and only a few PaK guns and Kempf, therefore, asked for all of the available Marders belonging to the Raus Corps in order to establish an anti-tank screen against Moskalenko.

2 - *Panzerzug.62, a powerful armoured train, was also placed at Raus's disposal and was used as a mobile artillery battery.*
3 - *The 168.ID suffered almost 4,500 losses between 15 January and 18 February.*

The "88" remained the best form of anti-tank defence for many German units, despite the fact that this gun was hard to conceal.
(BA).

Two views of the Marder II, with a 7.5 cm PaK 40 on a PzKpfw II chassis. This well-armed but vulnerable armoured vehicle was used within independent anti-tank groups, but also in certain divisions, such as the "Totenkopf" which had a Marder company.
(BA).

The latter captured Slavgorod on the 21st, not the date that had been planned, but being the only commander to achieve his intermediate objectives, he tried to exploit the advance of Golikov's armies moving out from Kursk. This threat forced the 2.Armee of HG Mitte to send a regiment to strengthen the left flank of the 168.ID.

However, despite Raus' fears, Moskalenko did not have enough mobile troops and tanks. Kravchenko's Corps was notably absent whilst it awaited a few tanks being repaired in Kharkov. On 21 February, the 167. ID dug in on Raus' northern flank.

Once again, the decisive action was taking place west of Kharkov. The 3rd Tank Army and the 6th army intensified their efforts around Lioubutin against the "GD" and KG "Thule". A ferocious struggle developed at this crucial road junction on 18th February. The following day, the riflemen of the 160th division attacked the "Thule" regiment before dawn, and using a snow storm as cover, whilst in the south, the 12th Corps tried to cut off the salient held by the 320. ID. The latter unit held on with difficulty, but not the SS. A "GD" kampfgruppe made up of a reconnaissance group, engineers, an assault gun and

artillery battery, stopped the attackers in-extremis in front of Kovjagi where the divisional field hospital had been set up. Other ad-hoc units intervened and by exploiting the lack of Russian reserves, stabilised the situation. The following morning, the Germans launched a more ambitious counter-attack and more or less re-established the front line in the 320. ID sector. Another attempt by the 12 Corps was shattered when the defenders managed to destroy the few accompanying Russian tanks. One of the latter, perhaps a KV, was destroyed in close-quarter combat, knocked out by a "GD" Landser using a magnetic mine. The Frontoviki maintained their pressure and with the "GD" in danger of being encircled, the division withdrew on the evening of 21 February. The "Thule" and "LAH" SS men covered this withdrawal. The "LAH", at the junction between the Raus Corps and the Manstein offensive, did not hesitate in acting aggressively. On 22 February, the famous "Panzermeyer" led his reconnaissance group and the II./SS-Pz.Rgt.1 against the surprised columns of the 15th fusilier Corps and the 6th army, inflicting very heavy losses. Meyer, who had already been awarded with the Ritterkreuz, added oak leaves to his Knights Cross.

The KV, vulnerable to the most up to date German weapons, remained a formidable tank due to its armour. It would appear that the one seen here has quite simply broken down! (DR).

All over, the Russians were running out of steam, whereas the Germans were attacking.

Also, on 23 February, the Voronej Front received new orders.

TOWARDS KHARKOV
THE COUNTER-ATTACK GATHERS PACE

Despite the 6th Army and the Popov group being hit head on by the Furor Teutonicus, Vatutin and the Stavka still thought that they could reach the Dnieper. However, the commander of the South-West Front was now asking for assistance from his neighbour, against what he still thought was a limited German action covering their retreat. Bogged down around Lioubotin in a battle of attrition for which he perhaps lacked the means, Golikov could hardly offer any assistance to his comrades in arms given the state of his mobile troops. However, on the evening of

the 22nd, the situation became sufficiently serious for the Stavka to order the axis of Rybalko's attack to be moved towards the south and Krasnograd, one of the jumping off areas of Manstein's counter-attack, although it did not halt the main offensive on the Voronej Front. The 40th and 69th Armies therefore lengthened their front. Moskalenko, the only subordinate commander under Golikov to have had any success, found himself with all of his units in the first echelon with hardly any reserves at his disposal (Kravchenko's 5th Guards Tank Corps hardly had any tanks left). Golikov was not under any illusions but had to continue advancing towards Poltava and Soumy, two totally different axes, a seemingly impossible task with six decimated divisions and mobile Corps[4]. Also, the 2.Armee was gathering in other units, including the weak 4.Pz.Div., which set up an increasingly coherent line against the 40th Army. On 28 February, with the support of the 59th Tank Regiment, one of Kravchenko's tank-less Brigades, and the 183rd Division tried in vain to take

Soumy from the 255. ID. On this date, the situation became catastrophic for the Soviet armies south-west of Kharkov when the German troops consolidated, like the "GD" which, thanks to the departure of the 3rd Tank Army, left the frontline on 24 February to be "freshened up"(sic) to the east of Poltava. Hoernlein's division got back to full strength thanks to its infantry battalions and various reinforcements. This was initially a brand-new second Panzer-Abteilung entirely equipped with PzKpfw IV tanks, a troop of PzKpfw III flame-throwers and a company of nine Tigers for the new "Panzer-Regiment GD" commanded by Oberst Hyazinth Graf Strachtwitz, an Eastern Front veteran and excellent officer. Also, in the face of the Russian pressure, Kempf carried out a new temporary withdrawal in order to help the counter-offensive. As for Golikov's mobile group, it stalled and fell to pieces. With a hundred or so tanks, Rybalko tried to break through a sector between the "LAH" and the 320. ID. The latter unit's numerous PaK guns were often enough to halt the Russian assaults and by the 25th, Rybalko

was reduced to less than sixty available T-34 and T-70 tanks[5]. The "LAH" in the midst of redeployment was preparing to join the counter offensive and remained very aggressive on its southern flank at the junction with the "Totenkopf". On the 25th, a KG combining Peiper's mechanised battalion and the I./SS-Pz.Rgt.1 caught the 350th Rifle Division by surprise as it was digging in solidly along the Bogataya River. The attack, as fast as it was brutal, reached as far as the artillery lines once the Stukas and artillery had knocked out the anti-tank defences. The SS claimed to have destroyed 58 artillery guns, but did not claim to have taken any prisoners[6]. The destruction of this strong-point further weakened the Red Army's defences against the coming German offensive, and Sturmbännführer Wunsche, commander of the I./SS-Pz.Rgt.1, was awarded the Knights Cross. On the 28th, in the light of the disaster now befalling the bulk of the South-West Front, the Stavka ordered Golikov to send the 3rd Tank Army as help. Its task would be to halt the enemy steamroller, especially the SS-Panzerkorps, which was moving up towards Kharkov after having crushed

4 - He stated to Kazakov, commander of the 69th army: "There are only 400 kilometres to the Dnieper and the spring thaw begins in thirty days. Make your calculations and draw your conclusions."

5 - On the 26th, the 320.ID had twenty PaK, including three Marder and 12 PaK 40, plus an ad-hoc armoured unit with eight Panzers and one StuG plus the support of Panzerzug.62.

6 - 47 anti-tank guns, 10 122mm howitzers and a captured German 105 mm gun.

This wrecked T-70 sums up the difficulties of the Soviet armoured Corps at the end of the winter of 1942-1943, worn out and sometimes equipped with tanks that were too light when faced with the Panzers. *(BA).*

**PzKpfw VI Tiger,
13./Panzer Regiment
" Grossdeutschland ", March 1943.**

Although the Panzerdivisionen still used a few PzKpfw III "kurz", the PzKpfw III "lang" and, above all, the PzKpfw IV, were an increasingly important component in their mechanised arsenal. (BA).

Another view, reassuring for the Germans, of an almost entirely destroyed T-34. The Russians became masters in repairing their materiel and a T-34 was often repaired three or four times during the course of its operational life. (BA).

German infantry advance across the steppe. Despite the losses, the infantry accompanied and efficiently supported the Panzers during the advance towards Kharkov. (BA)

SS-Obergrüppenführer Hausser is in command of the SS-Panzerkorps. (BA)

7 - The Kommandeur of SS-Pz.Rgt.3 was Eicke's son-in-law, which explains why he went to such lengths. This behaviour was not becoming of a high-ranking SS officer.

8 - The Corps only had fifty operational tanks left.

the 6th Army and the Popov group. The other armies of the Voronej Front, wich still had to undertake their vain assaults against Raus, spread out once again in order to allow Rybalko to withdraw and drive due south. The latter's movements, parallel to the "LAH" sector, did not go un-noticed and the "LAH" and Dietrich's mechanised kampfgruppen burst forward to attack the Russians. On the 26th, they claimed to have destroyed 11 KV and a T-34 of the 201st independent regiment. Finally, by the evening of 1 March, Rybalko's two mobile Corps, poorly "covered" by the infantry, reached with great difficulty their assembly areas with a mere thirty tanks between them! With supplies of fuel and ammunition having problems in following up, the advance was delayed for twenty-four hours under the cover of the 6th Guards Cavalry Corps, whilst the sound of battle approached from the southwest. Indeed, since 25 February, Manstein was pushing both the 1.Pz.Armee and the 4.Pz.Armee towards the north and Kharkov! The Panzers of the Heer and the SS now pushed back the 1st Guards army that fought back tooth and nail. During the night of 25 February, to the west of Lozovaya, with the "Totenkopf" reducing a pocket where elements of the 6th army were trapped, the SS-Pz.Rgt.3 sent forward a company of PzKpfw III to "reconnoitre". Alone in the darkness, without half-tracks or accompanying infantry, the Panzers came across T-34 tanks and Cavalry. They claimed to have knocked-out three tanks, but lost no fever than 25 Panzerschützen were killed. The crew of a PzKpfw III was even posted as missing along with its tank. Inexperience and a certain arrogance go some way to explain the terrible loss suffe-

red by the "Totenkopf" the following day. Whilst looking for SS-Pz.Rgt.3, that had stated having come up against a superior number of tanks before communications were lost, Theodor Eicke, the popular commander of the "Totenkopf", was killed when his plane was shot down whilst flying low over the Russian lines[7]. The SS armoured regiment was far from being in trouble, but was nonetheless fighting against a weakened, but combatant 1st Tank Corps[8]! It took two attempts by the Waffen-SS to recover their commander's body, who had been replaced by Oberführer Max Simon. The more experienced "Das Reich" was nevertheless experiencing dire difficulties in front of Lozovaya at the junction between the two divisions. The small town was an escape route used by the Frontoviki cut-off in the south by the Nazi advance and they used it to make their way towards the north-east. It was not until the 27th that the Guards of the 58th division were chased out of Lozovaya. At that point, the "Das Reich" had at its disposal 11 Panzers and 12 StuG. The Nazi "steamroller" could now continue its advance towards the north. On the right of the SS-Panzerkorps, the Heer divisions also continued to push back the remains of the Popov group. For example, on 26 February, the 17.Pz. Div. with good air support, decimated the 195th Rifle Division, only just missing the opportunity to capture its staff. This success also showed the weakness of the Soviet formation against the "Panzerdivision" consisting of two Pzkpfw III.However, despite the poor state of some of their units, the Germans were advancing everywhere. For the Red Army, the idea of advancing to the Dnieper had been abandoned and it was now more a case of holding

along the Donets. In order to achieve this, the 3rd Tank Army would have to gain the time necessary to reform the 6th army and 1st Guards army along the river. Thus began the last Soviet disaster south-west of Kharkov.

THE RIDE OF DEATH...

The 3rd Tank Army appeared to be doomed even before it was hit by Hausser's Corps.

Indeed, in the west, the "LAH" had gone onto the offensive and was "mopping-up" the few gaps opened in its lines by the Russian riflemen. This task was at times difficult. One such example being that of a small KG comprising of a StuG battery, a few Panzers and a company of Panzergrenadiere that managed to destroy three tanks and several artillery pieces, but at the cost of four tanks knocked out by anti-tank guns. On 1 March, the division launched a strong KG behind Rybalko's rear, with the latter about to be also hit frontally by the other SS divisions. The attack started well but then became literally bogged-down when a

thaw turned the surrounding area into lakes of mud. This new thaw was a reminder that winter was coming to an end and Manstein knew that the raspoutitsa would bring his mobile forces to a halt. Consequently, he ordered Hoth to drive towards Kharkov before it was too late with the "GD" that had ended its "rest period". In the east, the 1.Pz.Armee also continued its advance towards the Donets. Rybalko would therefore come up against a strengthened enemy determined to win a rapid victory.

On 1 March, the 6th Guards Cavalry Corps and the riflemen covering Rybalko's tanks, suffered their first shock. The whole SS-Panzerkorps was now advancing together, but, luckily for the Russians, the mud was handicapping the "Das Reich" and "Totenkopf" as much as the "LAH". Despite this, the SS advanced. At 13.00 hrs, the "Der Führer" regiment of the "Das Reich" stated having come up against an "energetic defence" by the Cavalrymen of the 6th Corps, but two hours later, captured their positions. The "Der Führer" regiment then came across another village held by a few T-34 tanks supporting the Guards, but this time the Nazi attack caused panic within the ranks

Although the PzKpfw IV was let down by its weak armour, its F2 version was equipped with a gun that could pierce any Soviet armour. It exacted a heavy toll on Soviet armour. (BA).

Another view of a StuG of the StuG-Lehr-Batterie that once again made the most of the low profile of this well-armoured tank. (BA).

PzKpfw III Ausf.L, SS-Pz.Rgt.3, Kharkov, March 1943.

This T-34 appears to have tried to conceal itself behind a house, but this did not save it from being knocked out. Note that some of the snow has melted. The weather was thawing slowly but surely at the beginning of March. (BA).

This view of a Sdkfz 222 highlights the particular shape of German armoured cars. They were still used, despite the arrival of light half-tracks that were better suited to the terrain of the "Russian Front". (BA).

of the defenders. The "Totenkopf" also noted such signs of collapse, but they were not generalised. On 2 March, once a few counter-attacks had been easily beaten back, the Germans encountered the 12th and 15th Tank Corps and despite the sticky terrain, progressively ate into the Russian lines. However, the "Der Führer" regiment became pinned-down in front of the village of Yefremovka, solidly defended by the Guards Caval-rymen and surrounded by vast wide-open spaces. Without the artillery support, which was bogged-down behind, the Germans were preparing to attack using the cover of nightfall, when a snow storm began. The Panzergrenadiere used this to cover the open spaces and approached the village from the west. Several Russian tanks, immobilised due to a lack of fuel, were knocked out by the StuG or explosive charges. When day broke, the SS "mopped-up" Yefremovka. A pocket was forming, closed in the north-west by the "LAH" and in the east by the "Das Reich", in which the 3rd Tank Army seemed doomed.

Its fate was sealed that day. Despite the arrival of supplies, Rybalko was constantly under Nazi pressure without being able to react. The "Der Führer" regiment advanced towards the west from Yefremovka to link up with the "LAH". Reconnaissance patrols had made contact the previous day, but the link was made more solid at 16.00 hrs when the Panzergrenadiere of both divisions established a real perimeter, trapping the bulk of the 3rd army, consisting of two Tank Corps and three Rifle Divisions. Rybalko soon gave up any ideas of regaining the offensive and ordered his units to set up hedgehog positions against the German kampfgruppen, before breaking out of the pocket. The 15th Corps, reduced to 17 tanks by the morning of 3 March failed to coordinate its defence, partly due to the death of its commander, Major-General Koptsov, during the fighting. At times, the Germans massacred entire columns attempting to flee, and at others, met tenacious groups that fought and died where they stood. They were also confronted with

Ju 88 A-4, 2./Kampfgeschwader 3, Ukraine, February 1943.

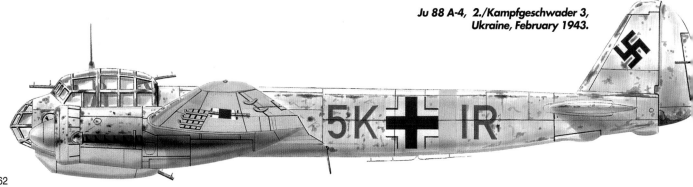

desperate attempts to break through the thin screen established by the SS north of the "Kessel"[9]. Finally, none of Rybalko's units were totally wiped-out. Part of the 12th Corps escaped led by its commander, Major-General Zinkovitch. The latter kept a cool head and when night fell, he made the most of the fact that the Germans were bogged-down, to escape towards the north. Rybalko escaped from encirclement as his headquarters were outside the "Kegichevk Kessel"[10].

In any case, the 3rd Tank Army ceased to exist as a formation. Thanks to some reinforcements, Rybalko established a new defensive line south of Merefa, making the most of the time that the Germans took to reduce the "Kegichevk Kessel". His "tank" army mainly consisted of the 179th independent Brigade with twenty-four T-70 and T-34 tanks, and the 195th Brigade of the 15th Corps that grouped together the remaining tanks of both Corps. On 4 March, the pocket was virtually air-tight and shrank until it disappeared the next day. It was perhaps during this last stand that the commander of the 13th Cavalry Division of the 6th Guards Corps, Major-General Serashev, lost his life. The Germans counted 3,000 Russian dead, 47 tanks and 159 artillery pieces, something that illustrated the weak condition of the Soviet forces.

With the last obstacle removed, Manstein looked to the next phase.

BACK TO KHARKOV

Indeed, the first thaws were a warning to the commander of HG Sud. Time was of an essence!

On 5 March, Manstein ordered Hoth to advance towards Kharkov. A new trial awaited the SS-Panzerkorps after a month of intense operations. The last unit to arrive, the "Totenkopf", had suffered due to its inexperience and had no more than 42 operational PzKpfw III, 16 PzKpfw IV and six Tigers, having started with twice that number fifteen days earlier. They were still better off than the "Das Reich" with its 11 tanks. Hausser asked the SS armaments services for an urgently required fifty 50 PzKpfw IV for the division, but there were none available. The men also needed to rest, even if the successes of the last weeks had boosted the morale of the exhausted Landser. Aware of the state of fatigue of his shock divisions, Manstein wanted to exploit his recent victories and make the most of the return of the "GD". On the right flank, the XLVIII.Pz.Kps lined up with the SS and also prepared for a last effort. The Russians were doing what they could to cover Kharkov with the German spearhead now less than 20 km away. In the north, Moskalenko, although he had the advantage of the Psel River, defended 120 km with three Rifle

Although it played an important role in defence, Flak was also used in attack, especially when mounted on half-tracks such as this Sdkfz 10/4. (BA).

Divisions and as Tank Corps. The commander of the 40th army placed three divisions in reserve to support Kasakov. Indeed, the latter's 69th army appeared to be seriously threatened with only a Brigade with ten tanks as its only mobile reserve. As for Rybalko, he fell back on the mediocre river barrier of the Merla, and the neighbouring 6th Army did the same on the Donets, although the Germans occupied the higher bank! Although the "GD" was concentrating behind the Raus Corps, the commander of the 3rd Tank Army knew that he was going to be attacked by the SS-Panzerkorps which, even before the Kegichevk Kessel was dealt with, began launching limited attacks to weaken the Russian defences.

THE BATTLES IN FRONT OF KHARKOV

HOTH ATTACKS ON THE 6TH

In order to surprise the Soviets, Manstein wanted Hausser to go round Kharkov via the west, maintaining contact with Armeeabteilung Kempf, encircling the city and cutting the defending Russian forces in half and avoiding long and difficult street fighting. The three Corps - SS-Panzerkorps, XLVIII.Pz.Kps and the LVII.Pz.Kps - lined up with the Raus Corps in the north-west, and the 1.Panzer-Armee in the east. For the 4.Pz.Armee, the "Schwerpunkt" fell to the SS. On a viciously cold day and on roads that were ice-covered or had turned to mud, the Nazi praetorians gathered their last strength whilst the Frontoviki, determined to stop the fascists from taking the city that they had liberated a few weeks earlier, prepared to sell their lives dearly.

9 - *The German name for pockets, whether they were trapped in them or were the instigators, was "Hexenkessel" which translates literally as "witch's cauldron".*
10 - *His biography written by R. Armstrong is very concise concerning these events.*

Soviet artillerymen with large calibre shells. At the beginning of March 1943, the Red Army tried to save what it could by preventing the Germans from re-taking Kharkov. (DR).

The photographers of the propaganda companies were very keen to take photos of Nazi warriors such as Kurt Meyer, who at this time commanded the "Leibstandarte" reconnaissance group. After the war he published his memoirs in a book entitled "Grenadiere" (BA).

The " LAH" led the attack, with Meyer's reconnaissance group still combined with the I./SS-Pz.Rgt.1. However, the artillery and most of the Tiger tanks were slowed down by the state of the roads and the operation began after a lengthy delay. Luckily for the Germans, the Russians soon withdrew back to a better defensive line. The Soviets defending the village of Sneshkov Kut , however, made the mistake of opening fire when the Germans were out of range. The PzKpfw III and IV manoeuvred and approached and took on the enemy guns. The latter and a few T-34 still managed to brew-up three Panzers. The arrival of the Tigers made a difference though. Their thick armour absorbed several hits and their powerful 88 mm guns pulverised the T-34 tanks and the anti-tank guns. The village was then mopped-up by the Panzergrenadiere and the advance continued.

The fortunes of war were kind also to the "Das Reich". Approaching a village held by the 253rd Rifle Brigade and the 195th Tank Brigade (with fewer than twenty tanks), it used its few Panzers alongside the 88 mm anti-aircraft guns[11]. They knocked out six Russian tanks and allowed the "Deutschland" regiment, well supported by Stukas, to take the village. The "Totenkopf" then redeployed on the left of the SS-Panzerkorps, at the junction with the Raus Corps. The latter was biding his time whilst in the east the other Panzerkorps were carrying out support attacks.

For the SS soldiers of the "Thule" regiment and the Landser of the 320.ID, the time had come to take their revenge on the 69th army.

7 March began with the arrival of ice-cold weather that reassured both Hoth and Manstein. Comforted by the success of the previous day, this time they engaged all of their armoured forces. They were met with success everywhere, except on the front of the XLVIII.Pz.Kps where the Guards of the 25th division fought for Taranovka until the next day before withdrawing. But in front of Kharkov, the Germans advanced and were not stopped by the river Msha. Thus, the usual combination of Meyer-Wunsche of the "LAH" inflicted once again heavy losses to the remains of the 12th Tank Corps that had been joined by other units. When the PzKpw III and IV of I./SS-Pz.Rgt.1 came up against a "Pak-front" around the village of Valki, losing three tanks in the process, two Tigers once again knocked out the Russian guns. The Soviet shells bounced off the Tigers' armour and some crews fled in panic, leaving their guns behind them and allowing lighter Panzers and the rest of the Kampfgruppe to take the village. As planned, the Raus Corps attacked the 69th army. The 320. ID in action alongside the "Thule" regiment, Panzerzug.62 and the 167.ID received no less than a Nebelwerfer battalion and the "GD" Tiger company. However, the main effort, of course, was provided by the "GD" divided up into three KG. For the first time, it engaged a Panzer-Regiment commanded by the "Panzergraf" – " the Panzer Count" – Strachwitz, accompanied by, amongst others, the Grenadier-Regiment. He came up against a fiercer resistance by the 305th Rifle Division, but the latter's defences lacked depth and reserves and the Panzers were able to outflank the Russians who withdrew at the beginning of the afternoon. The bulk of the tanks continued their advance with the Grenadiers easily mopping up positions that were now cut off. The two other KG also managed to break through, albeit with some difficulty. The slower Infantry Divisions met with less success than Raus and Kempf, but conscious of the mediocre Russian mobility, were not unduly worried. All roads to Kharkov were open.

The weakness of Kasakov and Rybalko's forces prevented any coherent defence being established south of the city. On the 8th, Hausser and Raus advanced without any great difficulty. Only the II./SS-Pz.Rgt.1 claimed the capture or destruction of five T-34 tanks and 30 guns on that day. As for the "Totenkopf", they linked up with the also victorious "GD". In the evening, the "LAH", with its 36 available Panzers, was less than five kilometres west of Kharkov. The manoeuvre continued the following day whilst Golikov attempted to hit back. He ordered Moskalenko to send his reserves to help Kasakov in the hope of hitting the "GD" from the flanks whilst two other Rifle Divisions, including the full strength 19th, dug in to the south and south-west of Kharkov, the defence of which at first fell to the NKVD 17th Brigade. However, although the SS-Panzerkorps had been tasked with going around Kharkov, Hoth asked Hausser if it was possible to take the city with a surprise attack given the favourable circumstances. Hausser, who knew that his star had faded by his refusal to carry out orders in February, however justified they may have been, wanted to make the most of such an opportunity. He therefore asked for clarification whilst at the same time issuing orders for the capture of Kharkov. Covered in the north and north-west by the "Totenkopf", the "LAH" and the "Das Reich" were tasked with attacking the city via the north and west. The following day, Hoth and Manstein sent another, ambiguous order. Hausser was to stick to the original plan....without neglecting to take Kharkov if the enemy resistance collapsed! Whatever the arguments in favour of one decision or the other, it is obvious that whereas Hausser acted as a soldier in February, in March he acted as a Nazi soldier. The prestige of re-capturing Kharkov would fall to him and his men, and not to the Heer infantry that was following up.

During this time on the flanks, the offensive was slowing down on the Donets as the Russian defence stiffened against the 1.Pz.Armee. Further west, on 8 March, around Sokolovo, at the junction between the XLVIII.Pz.Kps and the SS-Panzerkorps, one of the two KG of the 6.Pz.Div. came up against the Czech battalion well dug-in behind

Tiger I " 801 "
8./SS-Panzerregiment 2,
Kharkov, March 1943.
The runes are the
insignas of the
" Das Reich " Division.

11 - *Although the calibre was identical, the 88 mm flak and Tiger guns were different weapons.*

anti-tank ditches. They only gave way at the end of the afternoon, leaving behind 300 dead. Reduced to a dozen tanks and with some Panzergrenadiere companies down to fifteen men, the Panzerdivision had not finished mopping up Taranovka where the Russians were still holding out. Despite being worn down, Hausser's divisions and their 105 Panzers (10 March) were more than ever along with the "GD", the German Schwerpunkt.

However, the latter turned towards Kharkov itself.

THE ASSAULT...

On 10 March, the Ukrainian city once again became the focal point of operations. Three months after its liberation, Kharkov was transformed once more into a battlefield. Hausser's choice, whatever his motivation, surprised the Russians. Luckily for them, the SS-Panzerkorps spent practically the whole of 10 March redeploying or mopping up pockets of resistance. The "LAH" sent a KG to Dergatchi, north of Kharkov, in order to cut off the city. The Guards of the 6th Cavalry Corps halted the Panzers that advanced alone following a disagreement between the German officers. Disaster was avoided, but Obersturmführer von Ribbentrop, Kommandeur of the 7.Kompanie, narrowly avoided being killed[12]. A Frontoviki was about to throw a Molotov cocktail onto his tank when the tank behind fired an explosive shell, killing the brave Soviet soldier and

making the heads of Ribbentrop and his crew ring. The tank that fired the shot had no other option as its turret machine-gun was jammed. The Panzergrenadiere arrived at last and began clearing Dergatchi wich was also being attacked by a "Totenkopf" KG. Although the SS of the "LAH" strengthened their positions around the town, it was not until the following morning that the "Totenkopf" KG, led by its Tigers, controlled Dergatchi. Despite the day being relatively disappointing for the SS, the "GD" did not even notice the counter-attack by Moskalenko's reserves. Hornlein's division, still led by its "Panzergraf", was still cutting the 69th army into pieces on 8-9 March, accompanied by the 167.ID, 320.ID and the SS "Thule" whilst the Panzerzug 62 armoured train made its way along the track to Kharkov as a mobile battery. The Germans encountered few tanks, except on the 9th, 15 km east of the Bogodoukov road junction where Moskalenko's three divisions were concentrated and where the Tigers knocked out several T-34 tanks. Other Russian tanks returned the next day accompanied by riflemen but were halted once more by Strachwitz's tanks. These setbacks incited Golikov to withdraw the 69th army north of Kharkov, the defence of which fell alone to the 3rd Tank Army. Moskalenko made a few adjustments facing the German 2.Armee. Upon leaving Kharkov where he had met Golikov, he managed to make his way back to his command post and had barely arrived there when he came under air attack.

He managed to escape unhurt but immediately moved his headquarters.

The Stavka at last realised the scale of the disaster that had hit its two fronts. Vatutin was ordered to counter-attack the 1.Pz.Armee that easily repulsed the ineffective Soviet attacks. At the same time, reinforcements were rushed north of Belgorod (1st Tank Army and 21st army) and the 64th army was on its way via the east from Stalingrad, but all of these units would not be able to arrive and intervene before the end of the month. Around Kharkov, Golokov and Rybalko would have to rely on their own forces. The bulk of the 3rd Tank Army withdrew slowly south of Kharkov under the pressure of the XLVIII.Pz.Kps – 6.Pz.Div. and 11.Pz.Div. – whilst the SS threatened to come down via the north-west. The 10 March "delay" therefore allowed for some redeploying. In the west, the "Das Reich" was fighting against the 19th division and the 86th Tank Brigade. In the north, where the defence was assured mostly by the NKVD police, the SS pushed the 6th Cavalry Corps and two Rifle Divisions north of Dergatchi.

On the evening of 10 March, the commander of Kharkov, Major-General Belov, sent parts of the 19th Division to halt the "LAH". However, the real urban fighting did not begin until 11 March. Hausser persisted in his wish to capture Kharkov, even though the opportunity to take it by surprise was gone. He openly disobeyed Hoth when the latter ordered him to wait

until the XLVIII.Pz.Kps was ready to attack from the east, and instead sent the "LAH" and the "Das Reich" into the city.

Dietrich formed four KG and entered into Kharkov around 04.00 hrs. Moving out from Dergatchi, SS-Pz. Gre.Rgt.2 advanced in two columns along each side of the railway out of Belgorod. A first battalion was halted in the vicinity of the Severnyi railway station. The other attacked the Alexeyka suburbs on high ground, but was forced back by the NKVD defenders, supported by a few T-34 tanks of the 86th Brigade. A second attempt was made in the afternoon, supported by StuG and Stukas, but came up against a very determined defence. A T-34 knocked out a StuG, an anti-tank gun and a 3.7 cm flak half-track which was very useful for clearing rooftops. However, a group of Panzergrenadiere managed to get through the defences and making the most of the low number of defenders, took them from behind and wiped them out[13]. The two main KG entered via the Belgorod road. The defenders made the mistake of attacking when the first SS troops approached the airfield. The German automatic weapons caused carnage and the Russians withdrew in a rout, presenting the attackers with a golden occasion, preceded by a terrifying Nebelwerfer barrage. Making the most of the confusion, SS-Pz.Gre.Rgt.1 arrived at the Red Square in Kharkov around 12.30 hrs. T-34 tanks arrived on the scene but were knocked out by the StuG and PaK guns. The last KG, along with Kurt Meyer's group,

A PzKpfw IV "lang" with its wide winter tracks that turned out to be very useful on snow, but at the beginning of March 1943, the thaw began and the area around Kharkov became an ocean of mud. (BA).

13 - *Standartenführer Becker, commander of the regiment who personally led the manoeuvre, was awarded the Ritterkreuz.*

A column of German infantrymen in winter clothing passes next to a group of Izbas. Whilst the SS-Panzerkorps attacked towards Kharkov, several Heer divisions pushed the Russians back towards the Donets. (BA).

14 - *Untersturmführer Macher, commander of the "Deutschland" Pioniere-Kompanie, was awarded the Ritterkreuz for his role in this attack.*

strengthened by two PanzerJäger and nine Panzers, was tasked with blocking the north-east of the city. This got off to bad start when two T-34 took the KG by surprise, knocking out a Panzer and Meyer's armoured vehicle. The SS manoeuvred and knocked out the Russian tanks, then dug in along the eastern edge of Kharkov around a cemetery. The KG, out of fuel and cut-off, was attacked by Russian troops, but two trucks filled with supplies managed to get through before nightfall. As for the "Das Reich", the "KG Harmel", built around its "Deutschland" regiment, entered into the city as planned from the west, and the "Der Führer" advancing south of the city, cut the Merefa road. Harmel, despite the support of a StuG battery and all of the division's Panzer, in other words not much, was brought to a standstill at the edge of the city. The Russians had dug an anti-tank ditch, fortified the strongest buildings and deployed 122 mm and 152 mm Howitzers firing over open sights. Harmel soon decided to opt for a night attack. At 02.40 hrs, the first "Deutschland" battalion, accompanied by numerous

engineers carrying explosive charges and flame-throwers, launched a well-planned attack that overcame the main Soviet defensive positions, neutralised the bulk of their artillery, and set up a perimeter within the first buildings[14]. At dawn on 12 March, the mechanised troops crossed over the partially filled in anti-tank ditch. The flak guns kept the few Stormovik at bay and the SS repulsed the counter-attacks of the 19th Division. By mid-day, the "Das Reich" were nearing the central railway station when they received the order to halt. Despite the successes, especially those of the "LAH", Hoth was worried at the idea of seeing his "Schwerpunkt" immobilised in street fighting when the 3rd Tank Army was retreating towards the north-east without him being able to stop it. In the afternoon of the 11th, the commander of the 4.Pz Armee ordered Hausser to pull back the "Das Reich" that had been halted on the outskirts of Kharkov and, as planned, send it in a large sweeping movement via the north in order to cut off any escape route for Rybalko's army. The commander of the SS-Panzerkorps

Kharkov looked like a totally dead city in March 1943 and the Majority of its population had fled before the Germans returned, but it would not be another Stalingrad. (BA).

The "GD" received the very first flame-thrower PzKpfw III but it would appear that they were not used during the Kharkov counter-offensive. The tank seen here is carrying out a demonstration. (BA).

12 March 1943, a column of "Das Reich" on a road along the western outskirts of Kharkov. All day on 11 March, the division came up against fierce resistance based on anti-tank ditches. (BA).

hesitated, arguing that such a manoeuvre would be difficult, which was true, and waited until 21.00 hrs before offering to send a "Totenkopf" KG. At 01.15 hrs on 12 March, Hoth re-issued his previous order, to which Hausser contented himself with repeating his initial proposition... 15 minutes later, an angry Hoth demanded that his order be carried out. Hausser at last carried out the order of his superior officer. On the Soviet side, Belov, worried at the success of the SS,

abandoned a few buildings north of Kharkov in order to concentrate his forces to the east of the eponymous river, and blow up its bridges. Reinforcements were asked for, but only the 179th Tank Brigade came, launching a night-time counter-attack against the "LAH" in the Red Square and knocking out a 88 mm gun. The Russians had not said their final word. The real battle for the city was about to begin and would continue until 15 March.

A SORT OF REVENGE...

The conquest of Kharkov initially fell to the "LAH". The fortunes of war were still being kind to Dietrich's division. However, the defenders made the most of the terrain, fortifying already solid buildings and installing 76.2 mm guns in the cellars and thus exploiting the fact that the Panzers' guns could not be sufficiently lowered to aim at such low targets. Above, heavy DshK machine-guns were set up and snipers positioned themselves on roofs and upper stories. The opposing SS division could only count upon 23 PzKpfw III and IV, and did not have a single Tiger. It did have, however, StuG guns and assault engineers against the low number of Russian defenders. Consequently, its KG definitively secured the Red Square, clearing several buildings and, by operating in small inter-armed detachments, eliminated several strong points. By the evening they were around the Dzerjinski Square in the centre of the city. A small detachment reached Meyer, losing a Panzer along the way but bringing much needed supplies. A link was also established in the south-west with the "Das Reich" that had to wait until the evening before disengaging and leaving for Dergatchi. A single "Der Führer" battalion remained in order to mop up the south of the city.

Fritz Witt crosses a road junction at Kharkov protected from snipers by a Sdkfz 251. This photo was taken on 13 March as most of the city was under SS control. (BA).

This famous photo shows a Bordführer of the 7.Kp/SS-Pz.Rgt.3 and Grenadiere of the "Totenkopf" II.SS-Pz. Gre.Rgt.1 . One can see the fatigue etched into their faces. At this stage of the battle all of the men of the SS-Panzerkorps needed rest, but they were called on to make one last effort. (BA).

As soon as it was recaptured, Kharkov regained its place in the German logistical system and remained an important hub for HG Sud until August 1943. (BA).

The following day, the "LAH" continued its advance in the face of continuing resistance. Could it be that the defenders knew that they were gaining time for the 3rd Tank Army? In any case, the 12 tanks of the SS division were most welcome in order to support the Panzergrenadiere that had to attack buildings transformed into small fortresses, whilst the Russians tried to infiltrate behind them and attack them from positions that were considered cleared. Kharkov was not Stalingrad, however, and the defenders were very much alone against a methodical and powerful enemy.

When Peiper's KG had to cross the Kharkov river in the centre of the city, they came under fire from a fortified building. The officer deployed 15 cm sIG 13 howitzers behind the tanks and used these powerful guns to blow open breaches. The Pioniere then used their flamethrowers on the slightest loophole and, once inside, advanced by using grenades and explosives. Although their advance was not an easy task, the SS gained the upper hand. By the end of the day, north of the city, KG Witt took the industrial sector that had been ferociously defended by the NKVD police. By the evening, the Germans controlled two-thirds of Kharkov.

On 17 March, the two Panzerkorps tried to extract themselves from the eastern edges of Kharkov despite the counter-attacks, such as that launched by the 1st Cavalry Corps against the "Totenkopf" at Chugev. The state of the roads deteriorated as the thaw began.

The XLVIII.Pz.Kps and the "Totenkopf" finally found themselves stuck in this sector as their few Panzers were much needed there. In the meantime, the "GD" held firm against Moskalenko's three Tank Corps. Between 13-15 March, Pz.Rgt. "GD" alone claimed to have knocked-out 90 T-34 and T-70 tanks. However, the number of operational Panzers was also dwindling with only 40 tanks of which, on the 15th, only two were Tigers with none the following day[18]. But the resistance put up by the "GD" allowed for the arrival of Raus' two Infantry Divisions which encircled part of the 69th Army between Borisovka and Tomarovka, south-west of Belgorod[19]. It finally became a "Kessel" the following day when the Waffen-SS, appearing out of the east, pushed aside a thin defensive screen of riflemen. Despite the increasingly sticky mud, they approached Belgorod, preceded by their last operational Panzers. KG Peiper, with two Tigers and Ribbentrop's Panzers, attacked at dawn on 18 March under the cover of an air attack. The SS surprised the Soviet field workshops and secured the town around 11.30 hrs. An hour later, T-34 tanks approached from the north-west, but the two Tigers were awaiting them. A "Das Reich" KG arrived next from the south-east but came under attack from the Luftwaffe. When night fell, just as Rybalko's army had done, a large part of the encircled personnel escaped north under the cover of

darkness. This final German victory was more or less the end of active operations in the region. The following days saw little change and Russian reinforcements hurriedly dug in north of Belgorod. It was obvious that both sides were exhausted. The "GD" was relieved on 22 March, the eve of the beginning of the raspoutitsa which transformed the countryside into a sea of mud.

LOST VICTORIES?

What appraisal can be made of this series of battles? On the face of it, it would appear that the victory was a German one. Barely three weeks after the disaster of Stalingrad, the Ostheer appeared to have regained the upper hand, inflicting a severe defeat on the Red Army and removing any hopes that Stalin may have had for a rapid victory. Several Soviet armies had been decimated, leaving behind them 50,000 killed, a huge amount of materiel and withdrawing 200 km. However, the Germans were too weak to seal the Kessels as they had done in 1941-1942. They only took 20,000 prisoners and also failed to totally wipe out any large Soviet unit. As a consequence, many Russian units were able to escape and, once re-equipped and having received new drafts, could prepare their revenge.

As for the Waffen-SS, the new main component of Nazi armoured troops, as good as they were, with their plentiful and good quality materiel, they left behind them 12,000 killed and wounded in less than two months of

The Tiger tanks played an important role within the SS divisions and the "GD" when Kharkov was retaken. The Heer's elite division used them with great success against the Soviet armoured reserves north of the city. (DR).

18 - On 16 March, General Maloshitsky, commander of the 180th Rifle Division, was killed whilst leading his men to the frontline at Borisovka.
19 - Five Rifle Divisions and the 5th Guards Tank Corps – without tanks.

Panzergrenadiere of the "Grossdeutschland" with captured PPsh sub machine-guns, probably for the needs of the photograph. The division fought brilliantly between Kharkov and Belgorod against an enemy superior in numbers. (BA).

operations. The rest period imposed by the raspoutitsa was welcomed on both sides. Manstein regretted the fact that the mud prevented him from joining his forces with those of HG Mitte in order to eradicate the Kursk salient, but at the end of March, the Germans did not have any reserves whilst the Russians did. Indeed, the situation had changed for the Germans and the overall strategic outlook was disastrous. Manstein's victories did not erase the disasters of the winter and the loss of the Reich's allied armies. The re-capture of Kharkov did not amount to much compared to the shock waves and the consequences of the loss of Stalingrad which was the real turning point of the war.

At a lower level, Hausser's refusals to obey orders in March saved Rybalko from total destruction before large Soviet reinforcements could intervene. Hausser paid for this as he was overlooked when German commanders were decorated for the role they had played in Manstein's

offensive. The decision he made to abandon Kharkov in February was the right one as it avoided Stalingrad for the SS, but that of March was not.

However, this victory eased the pressure on the Nazi high command. Manstein, like Hitler, remained convinced of the intrinsic German superiority in mobile warfare against a Red Army that only knew how to win in the winter against the Reich's allies that were lacking in motivation. The re-capture of Kharkov did boost the morale of the Ostheer though. Manstein made the most of the situation to ask for permission to continue his offensive which could beat the Red Army or inflict such losses that it would not be able to constitute a threat in the short term. Kharkov once more became a Major logistical area for the Germans as part of a summer campaign centred around the Kursk salient.... ■

A 7.5 cm leIG 18 of the "GD" seemingly in action. By mid-March, the situation had stabilised north of Kharkov with the belligerents, halted by the mud and exhaustion, recuperating for the coming summer battles. (BA).

NATO SYMBOLS

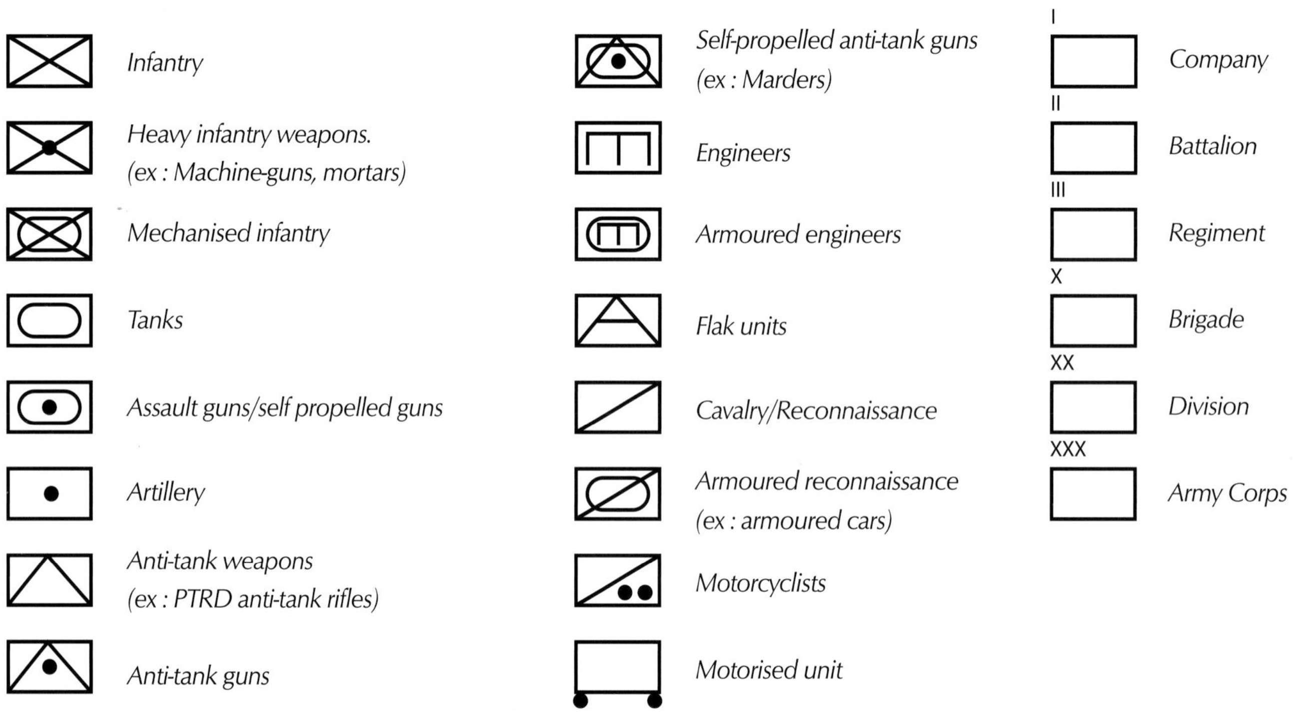

⊠	Infantry
⊠ (with dot)	Heavy infantry weapons. (ex : Machine-guns, mortars)
⊠ (boxed)	Mechanised infantry
⬭	Tanks
⊙	Assault guns/self propelled guns
•	Artillery
△	Anti-tank weapons (ex : PTRD anti-tank rifles)
△ (with dot)	Anti-tank guns

Self-propelled anti-tank guns (ex : Marders)
Engineers
Armoured engineers
Flak units
Cavalry/Reconnaissance
Armoured reconnaissance (ex : armoured cars)
Motorcyclists
Motorised unit

I	Company
II	Battalion
III	Regiment
X	Brigade
XX	Division
XXX	Army Corps

Notes :

The meaning of these expressions differs slightly from what is in use elsewhere and only apply to this book.
The terminology used by the belligerents is sometimes simplified or even misleading. The Panzer-Divisionen were often "Panzer" in name only, such as the "Panzer-Artillerie-Regiment" which had no self-propelled guns or even any type of armoured vehicle. The motorcyclist battalion of the Soviet tank Corps only had one company thus equipped.

◆

"Thanks to Myriam and Sylvie for their help and support".

BIBLIOGRAPHY

Armstrong R.N., Red Army Tank Commanders, the armored guards, Schiffer, 1994.

Dunn W. S., Stalin's key to victory, the rebirth of the Red Army in WWII, Stackpole, 2008.

Dunn W. S., Hitler's Nemesis, the Red Army, 1930-45, Stackpole, 2009.

Glantz D., From the Don to the Dniper, Soviet offensive operations december 1942-august 1943, Franck Cass, 1991.

Glantz D., Colossus reborn, the Red Army, at war, 1941-1943, University Press of Kansas, 2004.

Glantz D., Companion to colossus reborn, University Press of Kansas, 2005.

Glantz D. & cie, Slaughterhouse, the Handbook of the Eastern Front, Aberjona Press, 2005.

Glantz D., After Stalingrad, the Red Army's Winter Offensive, 1942-1943, Helion & Company, 2008.

Haupt W., Army Group South, the Wehrmacht in Russia, 1941-1943, Schiffer, XXX.

Jung H.-J., The history of Panzerregiment « Grossdeutschland » (...), J.J. Fedororowicz, 2000.

Maslov A. & Glantz D., Fallen soviet generals, Soviet generals officers killed in battle, 1941-1945, Frank Cass, 1998.

Margry K., The four battles for Kharkov, in « After the Battle », n° 112, After the Battle, 2001.

Nipe G., Last victory in Russia, The SS-Panzerkorps and Manstein's Kharkov counteroffensive, february-march 1943, Schiffer, 2000.

Sharp G., Soviet Order of Battle, Vol. I à XIII, Nafziger, 1995-1996.

Voronej Front, Colonel-General Golikov

40th Army, formed in August 1941, Lieutenant-General K. S. Moskalenko
- 100th Rifle Division (formed at the beginning of 1942 by the Archangelsk military district)
- 107th Rifle Division (formed at the beginning of 1942 by the Moscow MD)
- 183rd Rifle Division (Latvian division formed in September 1940)
- 303rd Rifle Division (formed in the winter of 1941-1942 by the Siberian MD)
- 305th Rifle Division (former-75th fortified region, formed in October 1942 by the Voronej Front)
- 309th Rifle Division (formed at the beginning of 1942 by the Siberian MD)
- 340th Rifle Division (formed at the end of 1941 by the Volga MD)
- 25th Guards Rifle Division (created in April 1942 from the 2nd Guards Rifle Brigade, honour bestowed in January, and the former-71st naval infantry Brigade).
- 129th Rifle Brigade (formed in the winter of 1941-1942 by the Ural MD)
- 5th Guards Tank Corps, Major-General A.G. Kravchenko (7 February 1943, former 4th Corps, formed in March 1942 by the Moscow MD ; T-34 & T-70)
- 116th Tank Brigade (formed at the beginning of 1942 by the Volga MD ; T-70 & KV-1S tanks, one company of vehicle-borne Riflemen carried in Sdkfz 251)
- 192th Tank Brigade (formed in March 1942 by the Moscow MD ; American M3L – M3 Stuart – & M3M – M3 Lee tanks).
- 59, 60th and 61st tank Regiments (9 February ; with each one in theory having 24 T-34 & 16 T-70). A Regiment of 24 122 mm howitzers, a Regiment of 18 122 mm guns, an Anti-tank gun Regiment (20 pieces), two heavy mortar Regiments (20 mortars each), a Regiment of 24 MRL, a Flak battalion and an engineer battalion.
TOTAL : approximately 90,000 men and 100 tanks- without the three independent Regiments.

69th Army, former 18th Rifle fusiliers created on 1st February 1943 Rifle Corps, created on 1st February 1943, lt.gen. K. S. Kazakov.
- 161st Rifle Division (formed from the 13th Rifle Brigade during the summer of 1942 by the Moscow MD).
- 180th Rifle Division (formed in the spring of 1942 Archangelsk MD)
- 219th Rifle Division (formed in the winter of 1941-1942 by the south Ural MD).
- 270th Rifle Division (formed at the end of the summer of 1942 par le DM Archangelsk)
- 37th Rifle Brigade (formed at the end of 1941 by the military schools of the central Asia MD).
- 137th & 292nd tank Regiments – the first was sometimes wrongly stated as being a Brigade, disbanded in October 1942.
- Artillery and engineers : elements of the Voronej Front reserves.
TOTAL : approximately 40,000 men and 50 tanks.

3rd Tank Army, formed in May 1942, lt.gen. P. S. Rybalko
- 12th tank Corps : Major-General M.I. Zenkovitch (formed in May 1942, by the Moscow MD ; T-34 & T-70)
- 15th tank Corps : maj.-gen. V.A. Koptsov (same as above)
- 6th Guards Cavalry Corps : maj.-gen. S.V. Sokolov (19 January 1943, former 7th Corps that distinguished itself during "Ostrogosh-Rossosch").
- 48th Guards Rifle Division (20 October 1942, former 264th division that distinguished itself at the end of 1942 in the Rjev sector).
- 62nd Guards Rifle Division (15 January 1943, former 127th division that distinguished itself in December 1942 during "Malyi Saturn").
- 111th Rifle Division (formed at the beginning of 1942 by the Moscow MD)
- 184th Rifle Division (formed at the beginning of 1942 by the Stalingrad MD)
- 179th Tank Brigade (formed in the spring of 1942 by the Moscow MD)
- 201st tank Regiment.
- 8th ArtilleryDivision (three Brigades, seventy-two 76.2 mm guns, eighty-four 122 mm howitzers and thirty-six 152 mm guns), two Anti-tank Regiments, one Brigade (72 launchers) and three MRL Regiments, three Flak Regiments and an engineer battalion.
TOTAL : 55,500 men, 165 operational tanks and 122 unavailable.

Reinforcements allocated to the 3rd Tank Army.
- 25th Guards Rifle Division (19 February, see the 40th Army)
- 253rd Rifle Division (23 February, formed in the summer of 1942 by the Volga MD)
- 219th Rifle Division (25 February, see the 69th Army)
- 1st Czechoslovakian battalion (1 March, formed in 1942 with Czechoslovakians living in the USSR, 941 soldiers of which 38 were women, it had an Anti-tank battery.
- 19th Rifle Division (1 March, formed in 1922, nicknamed the "Voronej Division").
- 86th Tank Brigade (1 March, reserves for the (Voronej Front)
- 17th NKVD Rifle Brigade (1 March, formed at the beginning of 1941 in the Moscow MD, five battalions equipped with light weapons and machine-guns).
- 113th Rifle Division (10 March, formed in September 1941 from the 5th Moscow militia division).
- 1st Guards Cavalry Corps (13 March, until 26 November 1941, 2nd Cavalry Corps, created in the 1920s and which distinguished itself at the beginning of "Barbarossa").

Reserves and troops at the disposal of the Voronej Front:
- 86th Tank Brigade (formed in February 1942 by the Ural MD)
- 150th Tank Brigade (formed in August 1941 by the Briansk Front)
- 2nd & 3rd Guards Tank Corps (arrived when the battle was over ...)
- 10th ArtilleryDivision (8th division of the 3rd Tank Army), a division of MRL (240 launchers ...), a Regiment of 120 mm mortars, a Regiment of howitzers (122 mm or 152 mm), an Anti-tank Regiment, 1st destruction division (two Brigades, with 56 guns and 250 Anti-tank Rifles), seven Flak Regiments and one battalion, three ski battalions, two engineer Brigades and two battalions, two bridge-laying battalions.

Total of the Voronej Front, 4 February, approximately 190,000 men and 350 tanks, without the 38th and 60th armies engaged towards Kursk. Some of the Front's artillery and engineers passed under 69th Army control. Artillery strength is, of course, theoretical.

Sources : *Glantz D., From the Don to the Dniepr (...) & Companion to Colossus Reborn, cf. biblio.*

Initial German order of battle at Kharkov

Armee-Abteilung Lanz, created on 1 February 1943, situation on 3 February :

- XXIV.Panzer-Korps, Generalleutnant O. Heidkämper, General der Panzertruppen W. Nehring (10 February).
- 385.Infanterie-Division (18th mobilisation draft, composite formation at the beginning of 1942, division incomplete and decimated on the Don in January).
- 387.Infanterie-Division (18th draft, formed at the beginning of 1942 in Austria, decimated in December and January and thus downscaled to a Kampfgruppe).
- 213.Sicherungs-Division (former 231.ID, 3rd draft, converted during the winter of 1940-1941, no artillery or anti-tank weapons).
- 298.Infanterie-Division (8th draft, formed at the beginning of 1940 in Silesia, decimated on the Don).
- 320.Infanterie-Division (13th draft, formed in December 1940 in Holstein, arrived from Brittany in January 1943).

Corps z.b.V. Cramer, Generalleutnant H. Cramer

- 168.Infanterie-Division (7th draft, formed during the winter of 1939-1940 in Silesia, incomplete and decimated on the Don)
- 88.Infanterie-Division (6th draft, formed during the winter of 1939-1940 in Bavaria, one regiment only present in Cramer's Corps).
- Infanterie-Division (mot.) "Grossdeutschland" , Generalleutnant W. Hornlein (created April-May 1942, from Infanterie-Regiment "GD").
- 1st, 10th, 13th and 23rd Hungarian Infantry Divisions and 1st armoured division (28 January : 13 tanks and two howitzers), all wiped out and of limited value.
- Sturmgeschütze-Abteilung.201 : five Sturmgeschütze, left the front at the beginning of February.
- Panzer-Jäger-Abteilung.559 : 24 January, 12 Marder, of which three were operational.

Total : approximately 50,000 Germans and 50 Panzers.

SS-Panzerkorps, SS-Obergruppenführer P. Hausser

- 1.SS-Panzer-Grenadier-Division "Leibstandarte-SS-Adolf-Hitler" (former SS-Division (mot.) "LAH" , created in September 1942), SS-Obergruppenführer J. Dietrich.
- 2.SS-Panzer-Grenadier-Division "Das Reich" (former SS-Division (mot.) "DR", created in November 1942), SS-Obergruppenführer G. Keppler.

Total : approximately 40,000 men and 280 Panzers – including 60 StuG and 18 command vehicles.

Reinforcements :

- 3.SS-Panzer-Grenadier-Division "Totenkopf" (former SS-Division (mot.) "Totenkopf", created at the end of 1942), SS-Obergruppenführer T. Eicke, arrived throughout February.

Note : We do not know which Korpstruppen – artillery, engineers, flak – were within the army Corps, but there were not many within the z.b.V. Cramer Corps and the XXIV.Pz.Kps.

German order of battle, 4 March 1943

Armee-Abteilung Kempf,, General der Panzertruppen W. Kempf

Corps z.b.V. Raus, Generalleutnant H. Raus

- 167.Infanterie-Division. (7th draft, formed during the winter of 1939-1940 in Bavaria).
- 168.Infanterie-Division.
  (Infanterie-Division (mot.) "Grossdeutschland", Generalleutnant W. Hornlein (created April-May 1942, from Infanterie-Regiment "GD")
- 320.Infanterie-Division.
- "Thule" regiment (strengthened), 3.SS-Panzer-Grenadier-Division "Totenkopf".
- One regiment, (strengthened), 88.ID.

4.Panzer-Armee, Generaloberst H. Hoth

SS-Panzerkorps, SS-Obergruppenführer P. Hausser

- 1.SS-Panzer-Grenadier-Division "Leibstandarte-SS-Adolf-Hitler", SS-Obergruppenführer J. Dietrich.
- 2.SS-Panzer-Grenadier-Division "Das Reich", SS-Obergruppenführer G. Keppler
- 3.SS-Panzer-Grenadier-Division "Totenkopf", SS-Gruppenführer M. Simon.
- 1 regiment, (strengthened), 46.ID (1st draft, formed in 1938, arrived from the Caucasus).
- 1 regiment, 153.Feldausbildung-Division (training, then reserve division).

XLVIII.Panzer-Korps, General der Panzertruppen O. v.Knobelsdorff.

- 6.Panzer-Division.
- 11.Panzer-Division

LVII.Panzer-Korps, General der Panzertruppen F. Kirchner

- 17.Panzer-Division.
- 15.Infanterie-Division (formed in 1934).

Sources : several including lexikonderwehrmacht.de